COUNTRY SQUIRE IN THE WHITE HOUSE

COUNTRY SQUIRE
IN THE
WHITE HOUSE

By
John T. Flynn

Doubleday, Doran and Company, Inc.

NEW YORK

1940

PRINTED AT THE *Country Life Press*, GARDEN CITY, N. Y., U. S. A.

A Warning

THIS IS AN ELECTION YEAR—*a year of campaign books. But this is not one. It is the considered opinion of one man only who makes it his business to keep out of the camps of politicians.*

The writer who sets up as a commentator on public affairs should keep out of party organizations. It is difficult enough to think straight without fouling the machinery with partisan emotions. The writer who joins the camp of a political leader ceases to be an honest observer. He becomes an agent.

But a commentator does have opinions. I have mine. For years I was the kind of Democrat who voted for candidates like Bryan and Wilson and Roosevelt in 1932. I was not the kind who voted for Parker or John W. Davis. I believe I may lay claim to being a liberal, who is well left of center, who thinks that the capitalist system may well be doomed through the unwillingness of its own defenders to do the things necessary to save it, but who also believes that its collapse in this country now would be the worst of all calamities. It is in the light of these views that whatever bias appears in this book originates. I mention it because the reader has a right to this check on what he reads here.

This is not a biography of Franklin D. Roosevelt. It is not an attempt to outline a system of measures for recovery. It is not a comprehensive analysis of the New Deal. It is an attempt to explain the New Deal in terms of the man who sponsored it.

JOHN T. FLYNN

New York City, May 23, 1940.

Contents

COUNTRY SQUIRE IN THE WHITE HOUSE

I

A Tide and a Name

THE CITIZEN WHO SETS ABOUT forming a judgment on a president—something every American citizen is called upon to do—must brush away many illusions, good ones and bad.

A president is a party leader. His own party is forever busy displaying him in a favorable light. The opposition party is equally busy blotting out these friendly colors and putting in others of a more forbidding hue. Both hire publicity men; both have powerful journals on their side. One party woos the imagination of the voter with ceaseless stories of the leader's wisdom, benevolence, courage and vision. The other as continuously exploits fictitious tales of his folly, selfishness, weakness and shortsightedness. In the end the figure that emerges is apt to be very far from corresponding with the flesh-and-blood occupant of the White House.

It is probable that no such person ever lived as that strong, silent combination of homespun wisdom and superhuman cunning known as Calvin Coolidge. The figure in the public mind was created by advertising, publicity, twice-told tales. The image that most people had in their heads and that they named Calvin Coolidge was as

completely a fiction as Lydia Pinkham, Father John, Dr
Munyon or any of the other characters of advertising fiction. One can get a picture of the true Calvin Coolidge—
the man who really existed, not the imaginary one in the
White House—by reading that delightful and wise biography by William Allen White, *A Puritan in Babylon*.

To be fair, however, we must recognize that much of
this fiction about presidents is not the work of paid propa-
gandists. There is the unconscious propaganda that newspapers, radio, movies and people generally carry on without plan or direction from anybody. Republican critics of
Mr Roosevelt are greatly wroth at what they call the "five
hundred newspaper publicity men carried on the pay rolls
of various New Deal bureaus, passing out daily hand-outs
to the press proclaiming the glories of the New Deal." But
they seem to me unduly disturbed. It is of course true that
the President has organized an immense battalion of publicity men in the numerous bureaus of the government.
But it is doubtful if all this army of puffers accomplish
very much for or against their chief. A far more effective
force is to be found in the wholly uncontrolled, undirected
build-up that takes place with very little external stimula-
tion in the minds of the people.

The office of the president is the most powerful on earth.
No sooner is a man made president than he is at once
caught up in a glamorous cloud of popular esteem. The
people generally pay homage to the great office. But men
do not distinguish very nicely between the office and the
man. And so the man himself becomes the beneficiary of
the esteem that originates in the office he holds.

He moves about amid scenes of power. Senates, courts,
diplomats rise at his approach. Multitudes gather to see
the human being who wields such power. Everything he

does, even his slightest whisper, is reported. If he speaks publicly, every radio station carries his words to every home. If he has a fine voice, like the President, the effect will be attributed to that. But we must remember that people gathered reverently around their loudspeakers to listen to the dry, rasping Yankee cackle of Calvin Coolidge coming through primitive microphones mixed with a heavy ingredient of static. If the President goes in his motorcar from one place to another, crowds gather in the streets, scores of roaring motorcycles precede and follow him, and a scene of great power and majesty is created.

Now all this may very well do the President a very great injustice and often a great disservice. It is inevitable that people get the impression after a year or two of this that the man who is president is a figure of heroic mold—a greater orator, a greater student and thinker, wiser statesman, more resourceful leader than other public men. They therefore expect him to do only wise and resourceful things. Having made a hero of him, they insist on his performing like one. They are prone to measure what he says and does, after a while, alongside this enormously exaggerated pattern of a leader. It is hardly fair to him. As a rule he is just a human being, usually honest, patriotic, intelligent and eager to do what he thinks is right and frequently as completely bewildered as any other public man.

This very excess of adulation and dramatization provokes a corresponding vehemence among his critics. His supporters rhapsodize about him, calling him the greatest of all presidents. Obviously it is in the light of this estimate that he is judged, first by those who hold this estimate and second by those upon whom it is imposed. Presidents get blamed for not solving problems that no man can solve.

That is what has happened to Mr Roosevelt. His opponents point with glee to the great army of unemployed, to the rising national debt, to the still suffering farmer, to the stagnation of business and a score of other problems that remain unsettled. The President's supporters reply, and with much justice, that perhaps he did not solve these problems but that at least it must be conceded that he has tried and with the best intentions; that he has done his best in every direction; that whatever may be said of the final result, he has been on the side of the poor and the underprivileged and, even though he has not been able to bring recovery, he has brought into being a number of splendid reforms in the interest of social justice.

This is a rational argument, and any honest-minded citizen seeking light will see the basis on which it is made. But this does not correspond with the picture of the superman who, we were told, was going to bring abundance. This description of a perfectly well-intentioned man who tried to end our woes and didn't is quite different from the vision of the giant of statecraft who was going to do it. The practical student of affairs will see at once the disadvantage at which this places the President. It makes it difficult for his supporters to claim credit for a good measure of performance because they had expected and promised so much; it makes it difficult for them to defend the President as a generous and well-intentioned person when they had built him up into one of the great statesmen of all times.

We shall all do the President—this one and all to follow —more justice and we shall serve the cause of the people more justly if we recognize that we are dealing, not with a superman, but rather with an ordinary man who, for the moment, holds vast power—a plain American citizen.

2

Franklin D. Roosevelt was born January 30, 1882. It is customary for biographers to add—"of a long line of Dutch ancestors." The complete acceptance of the assumption that Mr Roosevelt is "Dutch" is a sample of how this sort of error gets currency. It fits beautifully with the phrase that "he has his Dutch up" whenever he exhibits a mood of anger or resentment.

The original American Roosevelt, supposed to be Claus (or Claes) Maryenszen of Roosevelt, was a Dutchman who came to America sometime in the seventeenth century. Franklin D. Roosevelt is the eighth in that line. That first Roosevelt and his son Nicholas were all Dutch. But after that the dilution set in. Jacobus, the third Roosevelt, married a German girl. His son Isaac married a Swedish girl. The wife of the fifth Roosevelt, James, was English. The sixth Roosevelt, Isaac, married an English wife. Roosevelt's father, James, was the seventh. And by the time he arrived on the scene he was predominantly of English descent. There was only about six per cent Dutch blood left, six per cent German and twelve per cent Swedish. The remaining three fourths was English. James Roosevelt's second wife was English. So that Franklin D. has in his veins a mere three per cent of Dutch blood and almost ninety per cent of English blood. The Dutch name persists, of course, but the blood is British.

There is nothing unusual about this. The early settlers were Dutch but very few in numbers. They were quickly followed by large numbers of English settlers who formed the bulk of the immigrants in the first years of the colonies and of the states. Most of the old families—wealthy by inheritance—are strongly English, which accounts for the powerful English tone to the society that grew up along the Hudson and in Manhattan despite so many Dutch names.

James Roosevelt's first wife was Rebecca Howland, by whom he had one son—James Roosevelt Roosevelt. His second wife was Sara Delano, the mother of Franklin. The father was past fifty when Franklin was born, and the first son, James, was grown and married.

Franklin Roosevelt's youth until he was fourteen was singularly different from that of the average American boy. His father, a genial, pleasant man who took life easy and gave only casual and not too successful attention to occasional business ventures, played the role of a country squire. His estate was a very large one, so that the son was shut out successfully from contact with the children of the village or the countryside. His mother, a strong-minded, self-willed, aristocratic lady, did not send him to school. He was given private tutors until he was fourteen, thus being closed out from companionship with school-mates during all those years the average boy spends in grammar school. He was taken to Europe every year and spent a few months in a summer select school at Bad Nauheim. He was hovered over by a parent who gave him a mixture of pampering and discipline—the discipline of an imperious woman who wanted her own way even with her son and the pampering of a mother who wanted her son's affection. Perhaps it would be just to say that, when he first entered school at Groton, he was a good deal of a spoiled darling.

At Groton, his first school, he found himself in what is perhaps the most essentially British atmosphere to be found on this continent. The air, the architecture, the

ships directed his course. What practice he did was in admiralty law. But he spent a great deal of his time—more and more, in fact—as the successor to his father in the role of a young country squire. He put in much of his time at Hyde Park and, in the summer, at Campobello Island. He and his wife made occasional visits to Europe. And always he continued to buy naval pictures—engravings of old battleships and books on naval history. His tastes, his affections, his interests were all in that direction. He was never a reader of books. He did not give much of his time to the reading or study of history or the history of government. Such reading as he did was rather in the field of military and particularly naval history. But it would be a mistake to describe him as a student of these things. He followed rather a sentimental attachment. He followed a passion for boats, especially war vessels, rather than an interest in the scientific and structural elements or the technical factors in naval strategy. It was a hobby, a form of pleasure and not a field of study or research.

3

In 1910 the country was racked by one of those premonitory winds that precedes the main blast. William H. Taft was president and his administration was already well upon the reefs. His party was riven by insurgents; business was encountering various difficulties; there was a rising tide of rebellion against the ever-growing power of the great business combinations; the wrath of the people was especially furious at the "Money Trust"; the muckrakers were in full career. What was in progress—though none of these political leaders understood it—was the capitalist money economy going through one of its inevitable and frequent slowing-down periods. This has happened every few years from time immemorial. When it happens the popular leaders usually fix the guilt upon whatever convenient devil is on top at the time—generally the party in power.

In New York City and State one of the master politicians of our history was towing the Democratic party, with Tammany as his tractor. This was Charley Murphy, who was preparing for the state governorship campaign of 1910. Murphy skillfully managed to gather behind his ticket the strangely hostile elements of both Taft and Roosevelt. The angry attacks upon the Republican administration of Taft drove many liberal Republicans into the Democratic ranks. At the same time Murphy made a deal with the infamous William Barnes, the New York State Republican boss, under which Barnes permitted the scuttling of the Republican ticket in order to strike at Theodore Roosevelt. The wind was blowing for the Democrats. John W. Dix was elected governor. And young twenty-eight-year-old Franklin D. Roosevelt was swept into the State Senate on the crest of that wave.

I think we shall be fair to Mr Roosevelt if we say at this point that there was no special reason why he should be named to the Senate. He had taken no part in politics. He had had no career of any sort. He was not especially keen about the nomination. Dutchess County was Republican. There wasn't much chance for a Democrat. The city of Poughkeepsie was Democratic, however, and the Democratic leaders there were interested in electing a representative to the State House of Representatives. Lewis Stuyvesant Chanler, another scion of a wealthy family like Roosevelt, occupied the seat and wanted to be returned. The courthouse leaders usually named some

member of the "county families" or landed gentry to add
éclat to the ticket and get campaign contributions. They
sought out Roosevelt and urged him to run. He didn't
feel he had much chance of election and drew away from
it, but finally consented. He was elected, but not, as is
sometimes supposed, as a result of an attack on the county
bosses. The sweep for the Democrats played on his side,
and he found himself at twenty-eight a member of the
State Senate, swept into it by forces that he had little or
nothing to do with.

There he became a shining light in connection with one
episode—the effort of William Sheehan to become United
States senator to succeed Chauncey Depew. Charley Murphy had picked Sheehan as his candidate. Sheehan had
been the Democratic leader of Buffalo, Democratic leader
in the legislature and lieutenant governor of the state.
He was at one time national committeeman and, since
1896, a practicing lawyer in New York City. He was an
able lawyer and a master politician but a thoroughly corrupt example of both professions. Alton B. Parker, who
had been Democratic candidate for president in 1904, was
his partner. Sheehan was notorious as the political agent
of the utility companies and many other powerful corporations. His candidacy for the Senate was resented by
many leaders in the party—the liberal ones because they
were against the corporate control of government, and
some conservative ones because they recognized that he
would be a liability in the approaching 1912 battle in which
they scented victory.

In a joint session of the legislature 101 votes were essential to a choice of a senator. Sheehan did not have that
many among the Democrats. However, Murphy counted
on the power of the caucus to do the job. Under the rule a

candidate obtaining a majority in party caucus would be entitled to the support of all the party members who took part.

Of course the great strength of Murphy was in the members from New York City and a few large cities. The rural Democrats of the state were usually anti-Tammany. It required no special daring for an upstate Democratic legislator to be anti-Tammany. Young Roosevelt, from Dutchess, very early allied himself with those who opposed Sheehan. As the years have passed, the story has grown of how he was the leader of the movement. This hardly squares with the facts. Opposition to Sheehan was widespread. Even in New York City among Tammany district leaders there was a growing spirit of revolt. At least six prominent district chieftains opposed the selection. J. Sargeant Cram, one of Charley Murphy's closest aides and chairman of the New York County Committee, openly denounced the selection of Sheehan and worked actively for his defeat. Thomas Mott Osborne and William Church Osborne were the leaders of the movement in Albany. The fight took form around the name of Edward M. Sheppard, distinguished New York lawyer, to oppose Sheehan. The strategic object of the opposition was to get enough Democrats to refuse to take part in the Democratic caucus to prevent that caucus from ever having a majority of the legislature in it. Some seventeen Democratic members agreed to this. Roosevelt was one of them. So also was Mr Lewis Stuyvesant Chanler and the other representative from Roosevelt's district. As the fight progressed, Roosevelt was thrust to the front. His name was one to juggle with. And, to his credit, he took one of the most active parts in the fight. It consisted wholly in remaining away from the caucus. In good time it became

plain that Sheehan could never get a majority. Bob Wagner, Democratic majority leader in the Senate, told Murphy the fight was hopeless, and Sheehan's name was
withdrawn after a prolonged deadlock. Murphy then put
forward O'Gorman, who was promptly accepted by the
recalcitrants, including Roosevelt. The upshot of it was
that Murphy named the candidate, who was a Grand
Sachem of Tammany Hall.

Defeating Sheehan was a good job. The men who did
it were Edward M. Sheppard and the Osbornes. They
were well seconded by some seventeen upstate legislators,
one of whom was Roosevelt, who took a prominent part
in the job and who was thrust to the front for the value of
his name. It was a job, however, that called for no especial
courage or ability.

Roosevelt did not take any important part in any other
work of the legislature. He ran for re-election in 1912 and,
in that great Democratic year, was re-elected.

4

March 1913 the Democratic hosts, away from the flesh-
pots since 1892—twenty-one long years—were converging
on Washington for the inauguration of Woodrow Wilson.
Young Mr Roosevelt was also moving on Washington.
He had been for Wilson. He had made a journey to Tren-
ton a year before, when Wilson was governor of New
Jersey, to see Joseph Tumulty, Wilson's secretary. He had
ridden to New York with Wilson and Tumulty and talked
of support in New York State for the New Jersey governor. He became enthusiastic for Wilson and made an
effort to organize a Democratic movement for him in New
York State. But it came to nothing. He had been a dele-

gate from his district to the Baltimore convention which nominated Wilson and there had met Josephus Daniels and other national leaders.

Wilson was an intellectual liberal. He was a political reformer, enemy of political machines, champion of individual freedom and free enterprise—freedom, above all, from the restraints of monopoly, trade combines, trade associations formed to control prices and production. The great problems of the times revolved around these principles.

How far these problems had touched the mind of Mr Roosevelt, then thirty-one years old, it is difficult to say, since there is no evidence extant that he had given very much thought or any study to the subject. Generally it may be said of him that his interests did not lie in that direction. He belonged to that element in New York that might be called the "social welfare" school. It was made up largely of wealthy people who were interested in doing something for the poor with private funds. It was a reflection of the English *noblesse oblige* spirit—the conviction that those who were rich should do something for the poor. Under their sponsorship many fine things were done, many excellent movements were started—mostly charitable institutions, boys' clubs, orphan asylums, free clinics, neighborhood nurses, maternity hospitals, and all sorts of efforts by people of wealth to ameliorate the condition of those not so fortunate. It was based, of course, very solidly upon the complete defense of wealth accompanied by a generous sense of obligation to use that wealth in the public good.

I do not mean that Roosevelt himself or his mother had taken any part in these public charities. As a matter of fact, the Roosevelts—this branch at least—were not as wealthy as is generally supposed. Roosevelt's father had left an estate valued at $300,000, divided into three parts —one each to his mother, his half-brother and himself. He did not have possession of this money but merely the income from it. His mother had inherited a good deal more than this from her father. This has been estimated by some as a million dollars. It was probably a good deal less. And a part of it was in the large Hyde Park estate. This may seem like a great deal of money. But the Roosevelts moved in a society of enormously wealthy people who spent money in the most lavish manner. Their income, while seemingly large (Roosevelt himself earned very little), when spread over two country estates, two town houses and life amid the top-millionaire class, did not allow very much margin. Besides, old Mrs Roosevelt was a manager of the greatest prudence and by no means open-fisted. Indeed Franklin D. Roosevelt's immediate family has always been more or less financially cramped, keeping up a style of living imposed upon them by their neighbors and friendships within the limits of an income that may seem large to the average citizen but is quite narrow for the landed gentry along the Hudson. The President's own family—as distinguished from his mother's—has, indeed, always, until 1933, struggled against the demands of a social station without the immense income necessary to its support. There was, therefore, very little chance for the family to take very much part in the actual financing of the benefactions of the *noblesse oblige* theory.

But about 1912 the movement for compelling employers to deal more humanely with their workers had already expressed itself in movements for compensation laws, better factory inspection, child-labor laws, public appropriations for welfare activities. With these Roosevelt was in sympathy, though, of course, he had yet done nothing either personally or as a legislator in that direction.

He had not thought at all about the problem of poverty itself—how it could be prevented rather than mitigated or relieved. He was a reformer in spirit, but of an exceedingly amiable and mild sort. He did not feel any flaming wrath against the ills of his society. He maintained the happiest and most cordial relationships with the men who were being denounced by the more vigorous reformers of the Bryan type. It is fair to say that young Senator Roosevelt was pretty well satisfied with his world and had a gentleman's interest in correcting such obvious maladjustments as could be corrected without too much ill-feeling all around. He had already revealed that eagerness to have the good opinion of people—of all sorts of people, even of those he opposed. In the Sheehan fight in the Senate he got into no rows, he spoke no unpleasant word even of Charley Murphy, he fraternized on the most cordial terms with those who led the Sheehan candidacy. He was the kind of young man who could not bear to have anyone think harshly of him.

Up to this point he had been, seemingly, far from settled upon any career. The law seemed to interest him little. He had not been in any sort of business. He allowed himself very great leisure. He had been drawn into his political post through the importunities of the Poughkeepsie politicians. And he discovered that he liked politics. He did not care for research. He was in no sense a student. Politics afforded that easy-going mingling with people, talking, going to meetings, holding conferences, sitting around, making friends, having one's say, without digging or that severe discipline essential in the profes-

sions or business. He had been re-elected to the Senate.
He had been for Wilson. Wilson was elected! Why
shouldn't he go to Washington? And why shouldn't he be
assistant secretary of the navy? Theodore Roosevelt had
held that post. Now the Democrats were in office—why
shouldn't it go to a Democratic Roosevelt who was crazy
about the navy?

When Roosevelt got to Washington, what he wanted
was offered to him. Josephus Daniels had been selected by
Wilson as secretary of the navy. Daniels had asked Wilson
if he would approve the appointment of young Roosevelt
as assistant secretary. Daniels said he admired Roosevelt,
thought him "the handsomest and most charming young
man he had met in a long time." Also he said the assistant
secretary ought to be from the North. Wilson liked the
idea of a Democratic Roosevelt in his administration. The
day of the inauguration Daniels offered the post to Roosevelt—asked him if he would like it. "Would I like it!"
rhapsodized Roosevelt. "I'd rather have that place than
any other in public life. . . . All my life I have been crazy
about the navy."

The appointment throws an interesting sidelight upon
the course of political preferment in America. The Assistant Secretary of the Navy is a very important person. One
wonders what training or experience this young man had
had that supported his claim for this post. He had never
had any administrative experience whatever. He had literally no career outside a brief political one in the state
legislature. His sole work in private life had been as a
law clerk in a large office for a couple of years, to which
job he devoted but little of his time and that without interest. He had had no experience around the navy. He
had merely collected a lot of pictures of battleships and

some books on the navy. He was chosen, of course, because of two utterly hostile forces—Woodrow Wilson and Theodore Roosevelt—the Wilson tide that washed the Democrats into power; the Roosevelt name in New York that invested this untried youth with a special value to the Democrats.

He made, apparently, a fairly good assistant secretary of the navy. As soon as he found himself in that office he did, of course, precisely what you would expect of the youth who wanted to go to Annapolis, who collected naval battle scenes, worshiped warships. The world was in profound peace. But before he was on the job a month he began to clamor for a big navy. The Democratic administration, from Wilson down, was little interested in this, if not outright unfriendly to it. Roosevelt became almost the only exponent of a big navy in the administration. Secretary Daniels was suspicious of the idea as well as of the big shipbuilding and steel interests that were interested in the subject. So Roosevelt was looked upon in the department as God's gift to the admirals. He outdid them all. They took him to their hearts. He reveled in it all. He loved the big ships, had of course his own flag—the secretary's flag—that flew from the warships when he boarded them. He enjoyed and reveled in the most extensive ceremonials.

On April 11, only a few weeks after he was sworn in (when there wasn't a war cloud in the world), he said:

This is not a question of war or peace. . . . We are confronted with a condition . . . the fact that our country has in the past decided to have a fleet and that war is still a possibility. We want the country to feel, too, that in maintaining a fighting force of the highest efficiency *we are at the same time educating thousands of young men to be better citizens.*

This was more than interesting. For we find him here playing with an idea that he would nurse through the years—*that military training educates young Americans to be better citizens*. There are many who believe that some military training in schools or colleges adds to education a useful element. But that a stretch in the army or navy by itself, with its discipline, its stratification of classes, its living by orders, is precisely the kind of education for American citizens—that is an opinion shared by few American educators.

Later—and before the war appeared in Europe—he wrote in the *Scientific American,* February 28, 1914:

Invasion is not what this country has to fear. In time of war, would we be content, like the turtle, to withdraw into our shell and see an enemy supersede us in every outlying port, usurp our commerce and destroy our influence as a nation throughout the world? Yet this will happen just as surely as we can be sure of anything human if an enemy of the United States gets control of the seas. And that control is dependent on absolutely one thing—the preponderant efficiency of the battle fleet.

Our national defense must extend all over the Western Hemisphere, must go out a thousand miles to sea, must embrace the Philippines wherever our commerce may be. . . . We must create a navy not only to protect our shores and our possessions but our merchant ships in time of war, no matter where they may go.

Here—twenty-six years ago, before the World War was launched or even dreamed of—this young man, enamored of navy power and of battle squadrons, was talking about national defense. But he explained very clearly that he was not thinking about invasion, but about naval power upon all the seas of the world, great enough to assert our might everywhere, "running a thousand miles out to sea." Here is the forerunner of the plan to create a so-called "safety belt" running at places six hundred miles out to sea which was announced only last year. It still hasn't got out to the thousand miles dreamed of by the young secretary-warrior.

When the war in Europe began, Mr Roosevelt became immediately one of the most bellicose of the administration group in Washington. Among those who were frequent guests at his home and the homes of a small dinner circle in which he moved were the English ambassador, Lord Reading, who had been sent here to perform much the same service Lord Lothian is now performing—smooth and prepare and captivate American sympathies for the Allies. Another was the French ambassador, Jusserand. Washington at that time seethed with persons of all sorts —gracious and charming men and women of England, France and Italy, Americans of strong English and French leanings, officials of the State Department who, as at the present time, were handling the foreign relations of the United States while actually putting all their influence on the side of intervention. Persistently all these groups kept up that deadly peppering of American pride—"Europe crumbling under the heel of the Hun while Americans raked in the profits," "England standing between us and the Kaiser, while we played the craven's role."

The assistant secretary was in the midst of this and deeply imbued with the conviction that we should go in. Americans, of course, knew but little of it. They did not know then—and have learned only recently—how Washington officialdom from the President down was toying with the idea of going into the European war while Wilson was running for re-election upon the slogan that he kept us out of war.

When we entered the war, Roosevelt made two trips

abroad. First he went in July 1918, remaining about two months. He went to many places, visited everybody of importance, and made a visit to the front. He was taken down with a bad cold which developed into pneumonia and returned to America. He did not go again until January 2, 1919, when the war was over, when he spent six weeks there as part of the commission to liquidate the navy's war plant.

It was about this time—during the war—that Mr Roosevelt began to talk about a subject we shall reach later, namely, his belief in the principle of universal military training—a national army such as was used then by the Kaiser—conscription, in short, in times of peace.

The war ended November 11, 1918. At that point the power of Germany had been utterly crushed. The nation was exhausted, the Kaiser had fled, a republican government had been set up. Germany's whole war machine had been dismantled. Indeed the world was prostrate, save America, which still did not realize how dreadfully she had been shaken by her little-understood war prosperity. But not the assistant secretary. He continued, after the war was over, to clamor for more ships and more fighting men. On May 18, 1919, he was asking for a supplemental appropriation of $18,600,000 "to put the navy in fighting trim."

On February 1, 1920, six months after the Versailles Treaty had been signed in Paris by the European nations, Mr Roosevelt, making a speech to the Brooklyn Chamber of Commerce, said:

If we return to international relations as they existed before the war, we will have to spend far greater sums than ever before on the naval branch of the service, as the United States would demand more and more control or protection of its commerce, no matter on what sea. This might mean a cost of $1,000,000,000 a year for maintaining the navy. . . . This sounds alarming, but it is going to happen; it must happen if we are to maintain our national protection on an adequate basis, assuming that international relations go back to what they were before. I think it can be fairly said that our country will demand as a whole that our navy shall be equal to the greatest.

One of the strange episodes of the Navy Department occurred after the war was all over. During the war there had been an immense haste—ships, guns, war gear produced under rush plans at enormous prices. There was probably no alternative to this. But after 1918 the war was over; the utter collapse of Germany economically as well as in arms was a tragic spectacle by June 1919, when the terms of the Treaty were settled. But even after this the Navy Department went ahead with its war building program as if nothing had happened. The keels of ninety-seven destroyers were laid after the armistice, costing $181,000,000. There was of course no justification for this. Indeed there was every reason why the program should have been halted because of the excessive war prices and the rush character of the plans. Admiral Pratt was asked by a House Appropriations Committee about this. He said:

I cannot give you a real, practical, definite reason why, but I should say this: that if you start a big machine moving, such as this production is, it takes a certain amount of time before it gets slowed down and working normally. . . . We just got swept into it, and before we could get our breath and stabilize and get together, there we were in the midst of our output.

The notion that building ninety-seven destroyers is something that just sort of gets under motion mysteriously in the confusion and haste of the moment and that, before anyone realizes it "there we are," building nearly a hun-

dred warships and spending $181,000,000, is hardly a satis-
factory explanation of this phenomenon.

Ten cruisers, costing about ten million dollars each,
were also rushed ahead *after the war was over.* They were
part of the plans in the great war effort. But when the war
was over they had not yet even been contracted for. The
contracts were signed months after the armistice—sort of
slipped through in the general confusion and push that
had not yet slowed down. And they were built under that
fatal "cost-plus" wartime system that produced so many
scandals during the war. Many, if not most, of the ships
built in this postwar period by the department, largely
under the guidance of the enthusiastic assistant secretary,
were defective and many of them quite worthless. This
was, doubtless, inevitable during the war. The hurry was
so desperate. Destroyers were built on swiftly speeded
plans, and when they were built and took to sea they
were found defective. Yet in this postwar period, when
the Navy Department eluded public scrutiny in a country
absorbed in the dramatic collapse taking place all around,
these defective vessels were duplicated.

In all this there was, of course, nothing vicious in the
conduct of the young secretary. He was merely carried
away by his enthusiasm for warships. It was this which
made his office so hospitable a place for the shipbuilders.
Daniels was scrutinizing, suspicious. After all, Daniels
had been a businessman. He was the owner and publisher
of a very successful newspaper, which is a very exacting
business enterprise. But Roosevelt had never been in any
business. It is a singular feature of his career that his first
administrative post was one that involved the expenditure
of countless hundreds of millions and under circumstances
that suspended all the normal and necessary restraints and

cautions. Money was no object alongside of victory. And in the Navy Department, under his wing of it certainly, money was no object. In a speech later in the Brooklyn Academy of Music he told with a good deal of satisfaction how he had thrown money around during the war. On another occasion he boasted that he had paid no attention to rules, regulations and laws—that he had broken enough laws to be put in jail for 999 years. It is a fact of importance that in the shaping of his public career his first experience in administration should have been under circumstances where ordinary prudence, the rules of the department, the normal scrutinies of business and the very laws themselves could be daily thrown into the wastebasket. It made a profound impression upon his habits of thought and his methods of doing things. It was therefore quite a simple matter, when the war was over and the need had passed and the public attention was directed elsewhere, that in his zeal for war vessels, his ambition for a vast naval establishment, the "greatest in the world," capable of extending its power over the oceans "a thousand miles out to sea," able to defend our ships "no matter where they may go," he should be willing to slip over these hundreds of millions of contracts.

5

During these years in the Navy Department, Roosevelt had not been wholly inattentive to politics. He entered the Democratic primaries for United States senator in 1914 against Ambassador James W. Gerard and was badly defeated. Roosevelt made his fight on an anti-Murphy platform. In 1918 he was offered the Democratic nomination for governor by Charley Murphy, but refused it. By this time, of course, the whole course of that vigorous program of political reform and the curbing of power of big business that marked the course of Wilson's first administration had been swallowed up in the frenzied exertions of the war effort. It is quite certain that Roosevelt was but little interested in the economic dislocations that lurked in the vast military outlays and that would make themselves felt before long. His attitude then is reflected in his attitude as president, when he told pressmen that he considered the method of raising the money for a new billion-dollar preparedness program a minor detail in which he was not interested. His interests do not lie in that direction and did not then.

At the Democratic convention of 1920, which nominated James M. Cox of Ohio for president, Roosevelt was named as his running mate. There was in that campaign a feeble flicker of the economic issues that grew out of Wilson's first administration and of the economic issues created by the war itself. But it is obvious after reading the speeches of all the candidates that none of them had any understanding of these. Labor was interested in holding fast to the wage scales created by the war inflation, farmers were eager to keep as much of the crazy war prices as they could, everybody wanted to have all of the pleasant economic sensations of the war while at the same time being troubled as little as possible by its burdens. People as consumers had begun to protest against the war prices that had become even higher in peace. The population as a whole wanted to retain the profits and dividends of the war but be rid of its hectic and disturbing fevers. Harding's "Back to Normalcy" caught the popular fancy. But overshadowing all other issues was the foreign policy of President Wilson as represented in the League of Nations.

Roosevelt, as a candidate for vice-president, went about making speeches for the League of Nations. With Cox and the Democratic congressional candidates generally he went down to an overwhelming defeat—404 electoral votes to 127. The ticket carried only the Southern states and not all of them, losing Tennessee and Oklahoma.

Of course this was no stain upon the escutcheon of Roosevelt. The Democratic party was beaten before it named its candidates. There was a lively battle for the presidential nomination, but the vice-presidential spot on the ticket was not sought by any important figures in the party. The country was sick of the turbulence and controversy of the war. It was in the midst of the postwar slump. It wanted to get back to business under a business leadership. It was heartily sick of its partnership with Europe and wanted to become disentangled. It was disillusioned of its chivalric aims for which it had fought by the cold cruelty of the peace treaty and the selfishness of the victorious empires. It wanted to get on with its business. And the party of Woodrow Wilson didn't have a chance. With that defeat Roosevelt passed out of public life until 1928, when he was nominated for governor of New York.

II

The New Era

Roosevelt had resigned his post as assistant secretary of the navy shortly after his nomination for the vice-presidency. Defeated in November, he was now without a job. This was remedied in January 1921, when he took a place as vice-president in charge of the New York office of the Fidelity and Casualty Company of Maryland. He was given this position by Van Lear Black, a yachting companion who owned the Baltimore *Sun* and was president of the Fidelity.

Fortune magazine reports that this position paid Roosevelt $25,000 a year, which was the first large income he ever had out of his own earnings. He assumed his duties in January 1921. Then in August, while entertaining Black at Campobello, he was stricken with infantile paralysis. That seemed a shocking check to a promising career. He was just forty, handsome, athletic, vigorous, glowing with health. He was taken to a hospital in New York City and then to his home in Sixty-fifth Street. In about six months he was able to move about on crutches. In the spring he ventured to his office occasionally. For three years after his illness began he devoted most of his time to exercises, treatments and visits to Florida and later Warm Springs, Georgia.

However, he was slowly edging back into his business and professional duties. He formed a law partnership with Basil O'Connor. And he began to take a little interest in politics.

How much of a job his post at the Fidelity was, it is difficult to say. It certainly could not have taken a great deal of his time. Much of that was occupied with his cure, and he spent some of his time as well at his law office. One of his friendly biographers, Mr Ernest Lindley, says that at the insurance office each day he worked from ten-thirty to one-thirty, which included the lunch hour. He was away from the city a great deal of the time. There is a good deal of reason to believe that this was a job provided for him by an admirer. However, Roosevelt's name and connections were important, and it is a fact that the business of the New York office increased immensely while he was there. How much this was due to the influence of his name and how much to the rising tide of prosperity that engulfed the country, it is not possible to say.

It is hardly to be supposed that he gave very much time to the actual practice of law, either. After all, practicing law is a full-time job. And Roosevelt spent only his afternoons at the law office of Roosevelt and O'Connor when in town. But here again Roosevelt's name, his connections, his influence must have been valuable to the firm in that eternal search for clients.

The period covered by this adventure in private business and practice was one of the most extraordinary in the history of this country. The recovery of the country from the economic blows of the war was quite swift. The de-

pression lasted through 1920 and most of 1923. By the end
of 1923 the rise had already begun.

The reason for the recovery is important. The dynamic
element in the capitalist system is private long-term investment. This is a money economy. To use a homely and
oversimplified illustration, money flows around in a vast
circle in which there is a leak. It is the spending of money
that keeps it in motion around that circle. The man who
gets a dollar and saves it instead of spending it withdraws
it from circulation. The dollar, as it were, falls through
that leak into savings where it remains inactive. The only
way in which that dollar can be brought back into the
circle of active spending is by investment. When the saver
invests that money, he either spends it on buildings or
machinery or he lends it to someone who does, and the
dollar is back once more, traveling around until it falls
again into the hands of a saver. It is long-term investment
that brings the dollars of the saver back to work.

There is a great deal more to this theory, but it is perhaps better to leave it at this highly oversimplified statement for the purposes of this account.

Following the war several phenomena appeared. *First,*
all sorts of residential construction had been suspended
by law during the war. There was a tremendous shortage
of houses for the increased population, and this was accen-
tuated by the even larger increase in city population.
Second, the automobile had struck its stride during the
war, and an immense burst of motor building occurred.
This in itself produced a great new investment. But its
most important effect was to make a great change in the
habits and life of our people. It created large suburban
areas around every city. An immense building program
grew out of this. New streets and new roads to these out-

lying suburbs were necessary, public improvements, stores, all sorts of accessory construction. Farmers bought cars and demanded highways to town. Immense programs of highway building, carried on with borrowed funds, fed new funds into the economic system. Millions of garages had to be built, service stations, supply stations, filling stations, as well as a whole vast new industry to supply gasoline. The movies improved their technique, and suddenly movie theaters had to be built—twenty-six thousand of them, costing from ten and twenty thousand dollars to millions for the great movie cathedrals. On top of this, modern techniques in the construction of commercial buildings of all sorts led to an immense obsolescence of existing business structures. Modern buildings, hotels, apartment houses embodying the new elements of design and utility added to the flood of opportunities for investment. There was a startling development in machinery of a new type—handling machinery. The most astonishing strides were made in the perfection of the traveling crane, the lifting machine, including related engines such as the steam shovel, etc. This displaced a lot of poor hand laborers, but it created a whole new and virile section of the heavy-machine industry. Add to this the spectacular expansion of the electrical industry on every front and the billions required to finance this, and you have a picture of the kinds of business opportunities that called for capital and into which capital went. This was the basis of the great explosion of technological and credit energy that we know as the Coolidge boom.

It was inevitable, in a boom period like this when everybody was making money and had excess funds to invest, that skillful gentlemen, schooled in the techniques of taking the suckers' money, should find a paradise awaiting them. It was so easy to issue stocks, it was so easy to sell them. All that was needed was a little scheme and a few good names back of the scheme and a clever man at the tiller. One of the inevitable by-products of all this was the breakdown in our ethical standards. And one of the worst features of that breakdown arose out of this very search for big names behind promotion schemes. The promoter—usually a professional—had to gild his project with the sponsorship of people believed to be reputable, discerning, honest. For the man who had a good name—and better still a famous one—there was what was colloquially called a "nice piece of change" for the use of his name. Therefore hundreds, if not thousands, of half-baked, ill-starred and sometimes half-dishonest schemes were floated with two or three imposing names among the directors. This easy collaboration of prominent men and promoters in stock flotations was done either by men who were not nearly so meticulous in their ethics as was supposed or who were grossly ignorant of the meaning of their acts.

Mr Roosevelt had had no experience in business up to the time he was made vice-president of a big insurance company at $25,000 a year. It is altogether probable, therefore, that he did not understand the morals and techniques of the gentlemen in Wall Street. Despite his early association in politics with men who fought the code of the practical politician, it must be observed that Roosevelt has seemed to be surprisingly tolerant of certain ethical values in this shadowy world. For instance, the case of Robert Moses is one in point. There has been a sort of feud between Moses and Roosevelt for some years. When Roosevelt became governor he retained many of Smith's old cabinet officers, but let Moses, the ablest, out. There had been some bad blood between the men that arose out of the following circumstance.

Moses was state park commissioner. Smith appointed Roosevelt commissioner of Taconic Park, an honorary job. The Taconic Park commissioner was entitled to a secretary at $5,000 a year for his park work. One of the odd figures in Roosevelt's life was Louis Howe. Howe had been an Albany correspondent who had acted as clerk of the committee of which Roosevelt was chairman when he was in the State Senate. Howe went with him to Washington as his secretary in the Navy Department. Howe acted as a sort of political secretary—general all-around Man Friday and factotum—until Roosevelt left the Navy Department. When he was taken ill, Howe, greatly devoted to Roosevelt, rushed to his side and proceeded to serve him again, with but small compensation, as a sort of public and political liaison officer and secretary. When Roosevelt was named Taconic Park commissioner he sent Louis Howe to Bob Moses for appointment as secretary of the commission. This was quite all right with Moses until Howe explained that he would be very busy most of his time with Roosevelt's affairs and that he could not give more than a few hours a week to the park-commission work. Moses, who is a public servant of the most meticulous standards of duty, became incensed at this. He refused to appoint Howe and sent word to Roosevelt that he was crazy if he thought he could put his own personal political secretary on the public pay roll. This incident tends to explain, perhaps, the different codes of the two men. It helps also to explain certain attitudes of Roosevelt toward some of the grave responsibilities of the presidency that are mixed up with this more or less confused conception of public office.

To illustrate the type of promotions that flourished in those years of hot speculation, there was a project called the Consolidated Automatic Merchandising Corporation. It was a holding company. Its aim was to get control of various companies that operated vending machines. It did get possession of five companies that had various types of mechanical salesmen. These all-metal clerks sold cigarettes, candy, stamps, etc. This holding company, like many others, having gotten control of these subsidiaries and their mechanical retailers, proceeded to sell stock and to hold out to buyers the rosiest prospects of the rich profits that grow wherever the robot-salesman planted its metal pedestal. It tickled the appetites of its prospective buyers with the rosy hope of no less than 3,000 per cent rise in the stock in five years. It hailed the dawning of the new day of the clerkless store—that happy millennium when all the clerks would be out on the sidewalks while the mechanical salesmen and peddlers attended to their duties, and when instead of wages flowing to these displaced store clerks, there would be rather a flow of dividends to the stockholders of the clerkless store. Whatever the cause of the failure, the clerkless store did not materialize. For every dollar invested in 1928 the promoters held out the expectation of a profit of $1.50 (150 per cent) in 1933. But the profit didn't materialize. Instead of making the promised $18,000,000 in 1933, the company lost $756,000. The stockholders invested $11,000,000. They were told the company would have profits of $44,000,000 in five years—400 per cent of the capital. Of course this brilliant scheme, like so many others, ended in the bankrupt court. This is the sort of thing that could not have been sold without some good names to back it up. And in this case the original offerings were made with the names of Franklin D. Roosevelt and Henry Morgenthau, Jr, among the directors. The promoters sent out a circular with their offering saying: "The caliber of the officers and directors of this corporation, the wide diversification of their interests, as well as the broad field covered by them, is an advantage afforded by few companies."

One of the arguments for this singular adventure was that the clerks would cease to be wage slaves and would be able, after being tossed out of the stores, to devote their energies to "cultural progress" after being "freed from the deadening monotony of a mechanical job." Nothing was said about what they would substitute for the deadening monotony of drawing their pay every Saturday.

Mr Roosevelt resigned from the directorate of this venture when he became governor of New York. But his presence on the directorate throws some light on his mental processes. It may be accepted as true that he was as completely duped by the rosy vision of abundance for the investors and the delightful emancipation of the workers from slavery as any of those who bought the shares and lost their money. An eager, credulous mind and a disposition to see only the beautiful colors of any vision or any social or economic cure put before him, is a marked characteristic of his intellectual nature. It must be so. You cannot assume that he didn't believe the prophecies of this enterprise that he blessed with his name among the directors.

There was more than one of these adventures in Mr Roosevelt's brief sojourn in Wall Street. These concerns seemed to run to two types—one group based on the substitution of mechanical salesmen for human salesmen "who would thus be released for constructive labor"; the other group interested in exploiting the German inflation and financial situation. For instance, in 1927 Roosevelt and another set of directors organized the International Germanic Company. The directors met and organized in his law office. This company was going to finance German industries and buy the stocks of German corporations. This company too wound up in receivership.

Another promotion of Mr Roosevelt had to do with the airplane. In 1923 Mr Roosevelt undertook to be a prophet on the future of the airplane. It would be good for short commercial trips; the dirigibles would do for the long-haul work. He and others organized the American Investigating Corporation and the General Air Service to operate dirigibles between New York and Chicago. It did not take long to convince the promoters of this enterprise that they had guessed wrong. Altogether there were six or seven of these promotions, only one of which turned out well —a small company to speculate in German shares. It sold its own shares for German marks and then used the marks in Germany, where the value was still better than abroad, to buy German shares. It speculated for about two years and quit with a good profit.

Roosevelt had one other interesting adventure in business. In 1920 the New York legislature ordered an investigation of the building industry—the Lockwood investigation. Its revelations shocked the country. It revealed the presence in the building industry of all of those criminal combinations and practices among labor leaders and employers that flourish on so serious a scale now and are being pursued by President Roosevelt's assistant attorney general, Mr Thurman Arnold. Many labor leaders, subcontractors, material men and manufacturers were exposed, indicted, prosecuted and sent to jail.

When it was over, the building industry formed the

American Construction Council to heal and paint over the black eye the industry had gotten and to develop some form of self-government in industry. It named Franklin D. Roosevelt its president, and he held that job, along with his law partnership and his job with the Fidelity, until elected governor.

Here was an experiment in self-rule in industry as distinguished from government regulation of industry. On that subject Roosevelt expressed himself, on June 2, 1922, in reference to this council:

The tendency lately has been toward regulation of industry. Something goes wrong somewhere in a given branch of work, immediately the public is aroused, immediately the press, the pulpit and public call for an investigation. That is fine, that is healthy . . . but government regulation is not feasible. It is unwieldy, expensive. It means employment of men to carry on this phase of the work; it means higher taxes. The public doesn't want it; the industry doesn't want it. When an industry begins to feel that the confidence of the people is slipping from it, then is the time to get on the job and find out what is wrong. . . . The time is ripe for such an organization—there has been no system, no co-operation, no intensive national planning.

This apparently humdrum statement ought to be carefully noted, for here is that doctrine that we will presently see forming a dark cloud over American business. The doctrine was that business should be left alone to rule "its own affairs," that employers ought to be permitted to form into combinations to make rules governing the economic factors of the industry in which they worked. This will look at first glance like a complete contradiction of the NRA which he later sponsored. But as a matter of fact, it is the very essence of the NRA. With this difference—that at this time Roosevelt believed that business should be organized for self-rule, with a dictator or czar type of moderator instead of the government riding herd on it.

2

The next phase of Roosevelt's career sweeps him into Albany. He had recovered enough around 1924 to begin to take a part in political life. He made the speech nominating Al Smith for president in the convention of 1924 —when the convention was deadlocked between Smith and McAdoo, ending in the nomination of John W. Davis. About the same time he had discovered Warm Springs and began the cure there that brought him along to a stage of comparatively excellent health by 1928.

In that year the whole Democratic organization of New York State was geared to nominate Al Smith for the presidency, and Roosevelt was one of the most outspoken of the Smith leaders. After Smith was nominated at Houston, the Democratic leaders knew that Smith's religion meant a stiff battle. Smith had been unbeatable in New York State. He had served four terms. More than that, he had almost completely smashed Republican opposition to him in the state. Smith could have been triumphantly re-elected governor. But the Democratic leaders knew there were many people who would vote for him for governor who would not support him for president—some because of religion, some because of the aversion to Tammany in national affairs. The Democratic leaders believed it essential that they have a good man as candidate for governor. There was a good deal of discussion about this. Roosevelt was not considered at first. A curious fact confronted these leaders. Practically every man who stood out as available for the Democratic nomination was either a Catholic or the attorney for some powerful upstate power company. Al Smith was considered as big a dose of Catholicity as the state could be asked to take at one swallow and, with his power policy, a power-company attorney was out of the question. In this dilemma the leaders decided to ask Roosevelt. It is doubtful if Smith had any direct part in this choice. But when the decision was made, Smith undertook to induce Roosevelt to run.

Roosevelt was at Warm Springs. At first he refused. Years later he told Emil Ludwig that he was more interested in getting his right leg to move. He was edging away from the nomination. But it fell out that the plans of other men required Roosevelt as a candidate for governor. He had a good reputation. He was a pleasant person, well liked. He had never taken a very strong stand on any subject, save the League of Nations and a big navy— hence he had no enemies. His religion was right, especially since the Republicans were running a rather weak candidate who was also a Jew. He was an excellent candidate to capitalize on the immense prestige in state government that Al Smith had built up for the party. The leaders insisted. The day before the convention Smith telephoned Roosevelt again. Roosevelt still backed away. Then Smith asked: "I just want to ask you one more question. If those fellows nominate you tomorrow and adjourn, will you refuse to run?" Roosevelt hesitated, didn't know quite what to say. "All right," said Smith, "I won't ask you any more questions." The convention nominated Roosevelt the next day.

Al Smith lost the presidency; Roosevelt was elected governor. Smith lost New York by 103,000 votes. Roosevelt squeezed through with 25,000 majority. Both got about the same vote in New York City, but upstate Smith's religion, his stand on prohibition, his Tammany connections lost him votes he was always able to command in a state fight. Roosevelt obviously had no such handicap. He was running against a weak candidate and the first Jew to run for governor of New York. And Roosevelt had never opposed prohibition. Mrs Roosevelt had been an active Dry, and Roosevelt himself had always dodged the issue.

Roosevelt served two terms as governor of New York. By 1930, however, the great Hoover depression was in full swing. The Republican party was badly discredited, and the New York City Democratic scandals had hardly yet advanced to a critical stage.

It is a curious fact that Roosevelt's stay in Albany was so generally critically unobserved. This was probably due to the fact that the depression was a national question and so completely engrossed public attention that affairs in Albany remained more or less unnoticed. There was nothing at all spectacular about Roosevelt's regime. Generally he followed Al Smith's policies. He had a good record in pressing for the social reforms that Smith had initiated—the 48-hour week for women and children, extension of workmen's compensation, limitation on temporary injunctions in labor disputes, study of old-age security and the like.

During his tenure as governor all that seemingly new and bewildering range of problems growing out of the depression took shape and spread and engulfed the various governments—relief, unemployment, taxes, deficits, bank and business failures, financial scandals. But Roosevelt gave very little evidence of being aware of the seriousness of the era into which we were plunging.

Just before the crash he saw everything "in a very healthy and prosperous condition." After the crash he spoke of it as a mere passing event that affected only those who had tried to gamble. The attitude and philosophy he improvised about this growing disaster we can examine later. The truth is that the vision of the White House that filled Roosevelt's mind after Smith's defeat and his own election flamed up into a passion after the depression had progressed far enough to discredit Hoover. From then on his mind and attention were occupied mostly with his candidacy for the presidency.

An excellent example of this is found in his messages to the legislature. One has but to compare, say, his message of 1931 with that of Al Smith in 1928. Smith's message is a detailed analysis of the problems, the activities, the finances of the commonwealth covering almost a hundred pages and affording any legislator or citizen an illuminating picture of its affairs. Roosevelt's message comprised thirteen and a half pages, one succession of generalities after another, apparently dashed off by some subordinate and, in a period of grave financial disturbance, containing not one word about the finances of the state. The two messages are characteristic of the two men as governor.

3

An incident in the banking world enables us to have a look at another facet of Roosevelt's mental processes at this time. The City Trust Company failed in New York City. Lieutenant Governor Lehman, in Roosevelt's absence, appointed Robert Moses to investigate the ensuing scandal. Moses condemned thrift accounts and bank affiliates. He pointed to the Bank of the United States as a shining example of these evils. When Roosevelt returned he ignored the Moses report. Instead he named a commission to study the subject and he put a director of the *Bank of the United States on the commission*. Of course the commission did nothing. It made an innocuous report. A few months later the Bank of the United States failed in one of the most smelly disasters of the whole banking episode.

Now the significant point in this is that Roosevelt cordially had disliked Robert Moses ever since the incident in which Moses angrily refused to carry Roosevelt's own private secretary on the public pay roll. That was sufficient to influence Roosevelt to completely ignore not only Moses' report but the grave banking condition to which it called attention. The President's mind is powerfully influenced upon the most serious matters by his likes and dislikes. He does not dislike many people. He is inclined to be friendly with everyone. But where the personal element enters the equation, it is invariably the controlling one. The other interesting mental indicator here is to be found in his appointment of a director of the Bank of the United States on a commission to investigate a condition of which that bank was supposed to be the worst exemplar. For some reason which it is difficult to understand, he does not perceive the impropriety of this practice— there is some blind spot or mental obfuscation on the point that is not easily explained.

The problems of bank affiliates was to become one of the most scandalous in the whole banking world. Yet Roosevelt as governor, even after the Bank of the United States failure, never did anything about them. When he was president they were ended by a Federal act. But he had nothing to do with it. It was accomplished by a bill introduced by Senator Carter Glass to which Roosevelt strangely refused to lend his aid.

When Al Smith turned over the state's affairs to Roosevelt, there were appropriations and funds to take care of all the state's commitments until December 31, 1930, and a surplus of $15,000,000 in cash besides. When Roosevelt left the governor's office December 31, 1932, the state had a deficit of $90,000,000. The explanation of this, of course, must be sought partly in the depression with its attendant reduction of revenues, but also in the governor's failure to increase revenues while curtailing the state's outlays. Many governors, however, committed the same mistake.

What it is not so easy to understand is that while he was thus piling up deficits for the state, he was roundly denouncing Hoover, who was doing the same thing for the nation.

The depression deepened, the skies darkened, but the governor maintained his glowing good humor. He talked to a meeting of governors in Salt Lake City about unemployment insurance but did not seem to consider it of pressing importance—something ought to be done, but haste was unwise. He was opposed to direct relief because it was a dole and he feared its "character-destroying" aspect.

To a man of the governor's temperament, irked by the hard, dry realities of finance and administration, it was quite natural that the vision of the White House and the excitement of the approaching political contest should usurp his attention. As the months rolled by and recovery resisted all the enticements of Herbert Hoover, as the bread lines lengthened and profits vanished, Republican prospects of victory receded and the value of the Democratic nomination became ever more enhanced. Jim

Farley, Democratic state chairman, thrust into that post by Smith, was touring the country seeking Roosevelt delegates. One of the early acts of the governor was to set up a publicity department in Albany to advertise the achievements of his administration and those, in particular, of its chief, Franklin D. Roosevelt.

The prohibition problem began to bother him. He had managed to keep mum on it, but prohibition, like many other things, was being blown away by the strange winds of the depression. In the campaign of 1930 for re-election he still evaded the question. Mrs Roosevelt's well-known Dry allegiance and the governor's silence were used to hold the Dry vote. He was urged to state his position on the question. He replied that he was elected on a platform that stated the party's position on the question, his term was not yet expired, the party would define its position when it adopted its platform and until then there "was logically no need for me to define state issues." But as the campaign approached he heard that Charles H. Tuttle would be the Republican nominee and would declare for repeal. By this time prohibition was generally condemned and doomed. The men who for years had fought it and finally broken its back and been ruined in their battles were out of the picture. Roosevelt, who had at first supported it, then kept quiet about it, stepped in to enjoy the rewards of repeal.

One other subject dogged his footsteps. Charley Murphy was dead. The discipline to which he had subjected Tammany was gone. Under Jimmy Walker's leadership it had slipped back to the low estate of its worst days. Scandals began to explode here and there. They touched the Bench first. In the midst of this a bill was introduced, sponsored by the Brooklyn McCooey machine, providing for four new judges in Brooklyn. The Republicans balked because McCooey was sure to elect all four judges. This unhappy state of affairs was neatly settled by one of those famous bipartisan deals for which New York City is famous. The bill was changed to provide for twelve judges instead of four—seven to be in Democratic-controlled districts and five in Republican districts. Lawyers, citizens protested against this deal. But Roosevelt signed the bill. Moreover, he admitted he had heard of the deal and observed that if the people didn't like the judges the bosses picked for them they could choose others. He was still hoping he might have the New York delegation.

This whole subject involved the question of Roosevelt's relationships with the Tammany politicians. He has been very severely criticized by liberal and reform groups for what are called his efforts to save Tammany corruptionists from the investigation that finally ruined them. The whole subject is a little involved. In all fairness it must be said that Roosevelt faced a difficult situation. He was a candidate for president. The votes of the New York delegation would be important to him. Tammany controlled an immense section of those votes. But New York City was overrun with grafters—crooked judges, crooked commissioners, scandals becoming more and more nauseous. It was difficult to traffic with these men without becoming stained by them. They were making Roosevelt's position very difficult. He was laboring with great difficulty, posing as the enemy of corrupt machines while hoping to hold their votes.

At the same time the Republicans were making every effort to put him on the spot by clamoring for action. Following grave judicial scandals, the Republican legislature passed a bill authorizing Roosevelt to investigate conditions in New York City. He vetoed it. Then came the exposures following Supreme Court Justice Vause and the pier scandals. Newspapers demanded that Roosevelt name a Moreland commissioner to investigate. Again he ducked the issue. As one shocking episode followed another, the governor continued to find new excuses for resisting investigation. The state campaign of 1930 opened. Tuttle, candidate for governor, nightly denounced Roosevelt for his tolerance in the presence of the New York City scandals. He was finally driven by this attack to ask the Appellate Court to investigate the magistrates.

Then a grand jury began investigation of the notorious Magistrate Ewald case. Democratic leaders, including Boss Curry and Mayor Walker, refused to waive immunity. The prosecutor appealed to Roosevelt. Roosevelt wrote Walker a letter saying "No man should hold public office and refuse to waive immunity with respect to his *public* [italics mine] acts." This had the sound of high public virtue, but it was an artfully phrased sentence. These leaders were being questioned, not about their strictly public acts, but about all sorts of scandalous private transactions in which they were alleged to have engaged. They promptly announced themselves ready to waive immunity for their public acts but still refused to testify. Liberal groups in New York said Roosevelt had saved them again.

The City Affairs Committee and the City Club of New York filed with the governor charges against Mayor Walker and Judge Crain—detailed, particularized, covering fifteen pages. Roosevelt did nothing. He referred the charges against Walker to Walker for a reply and refused the City Affairs Committee an opportunity to refute Walker's reply and then dismissed the whole thing as too general.

Then the legislature in 1931 ordered the famous Hofstadter investigation, with Judge Samuel Seabury as its counsel. The amazing disclosures of Seabury, which alternately shocked and amused the country, presented a new difficulty for Roosevelt. Seabury was exposing the famous tin-box brigade. One member of it was Sheriff Thomas Farley, whose tin box was loaded with cash he refused to explain. Roosevelt took no notice of this. At the end of three months Seabury asked Roosevelt to take action on it. Again he did nothing. A month later—January 18, 1932—the Committee of One Thousand and the City Affairs Committee of New York put the case up to Roosevelt in the form of definite charges against Farley. It took nearly four months to get Roosevelt to act. His liberal supporters grew troubled. It was then that he put Farley on trial and removed him, with a statement that has become famous. That statement is that as a matter of public policy an official who is under investigation and whose scale of living or bank deposits exceed his public salary "owes a positive public duty to the community to give a reasonable or credible explanation of the deposits or the source which enables him to maintain a scale of living beyond the amount of his salary." This statement was written by Raymond Moley, who by this time had been called in as the organizer of Roosevelt's brain trust.

Following this statement Rabbi Stephen Wise and Dr John Haynes Holmes, of the City Affairs Committee, two outstanding citizens of New York, made up a record of charges against Sheriff James McQuade of Queens County and John Theofel, chief clerk of the Surrogate's Court in Queens. Both had large bank deposits, and McQuade had become almost a national comic figure as a result of Seabury's scorching examination of him. This time Roosevelt lost his temper, but not about McQuade or the grafters, but against Dr Holmes and Dr Wise. He accused them of grave impropriety in asking him to exert pressure "on a high judicial officer."

Roosevelt filled some of the vacancies caused by the Seabury investigation on the recommendation of Boss Curry. When Wise and Holmes complained about Roosevelt's refusal to act, Roosevelt answered tartly: "If they would serve their God as they seek to serve themselves the people of the City of New York would be the gainers."

In the end Seabury put Mayor Walker on the stand, grilled him mercilessly. The testimony was damning, but again Roosevelt refused to act. Seabury then filed charges. The Democratic convention was about to meet. Roosevelt was fencing to put the ordeal off until after the convention. The battle for control of that New York delegation ruled by the New York gang was still on. Finally, in early June, Seabury made formal charges before Roosevelt against Walker. Roosevelt sent the charges to Walker and put the trial off until after the convention.

Roosevelt put Walker on trial in August. By this time he had been nominated for the presidency. He had suffered severely in the eyes of the reform groups in New York, but he made a good showing during the trial of Walker. In this case, at the suggestion of Raymond Moley, Roosevelt asked Martin Conboy to act as his counsel. Conboy is an able, experienced and studious lawyer. He digested the evidence, sat at Roosevelt's elbow, prepared the questions for him and generally coached him. As Walker testified before Roosevelt, his case became darker and more difficult. Many people began to wonder why Roosevelt did not act. There is still some doubt as to what Roosevelt would have done. It is known that he had expressed some question as to whether he ought to remove Walker. The campaign was on, the Democratic party in New York City was in the hands of Walker's sponsors, the vote of New York in the election was important to him. In the midst of this Walker resigned.

After that Roosevelt plunged into the campaign for the presidency, and for all practical purposes his services as governor were at an end.

A fair estimate of Roosevelt as governor would be that he had been a fair executive but in no sense a brilliant one. He had an excellent record in his support of those policies for social justice for the workers and the poor that had been initiated by Smith, but he did not have much success in passing the laws he supported. He did not get along well with the legislature. Like Smith he had to contend with Republican majorities. And he did not seem to know how to get out of them as much as Smith did. While his record on social justice was good, his record on finance was quite bad. In his last year he had a deficit of $48,000,000 and had put the state in the red to the extent of nearly $90,000,000. He had increased the bonded indebtedness by $111,000,000. He had surprised many liberals by his veto of a civil-service bill passed by the legislature. He had really given more time to the campaign for the presidency than to the management of the state. He had displayed a singular complacence about the spreading economic wreckage all about him. On the other hand he had had a good record on power. He had generally followed Smith's lead in asserting the right of the people of the state to the ownership of their rich water-power resources and the wisdom of having the state generate the power and sell it to private companies for distribution at the power plant, thus holding over the heads of the distributors as a weapon for fair rates the power to control the current at the spiggot. Liberals generally approved this course. But on the whole, despite his good record on subjects like old-age pensions, labor laws, etc., they were far from pleased with him. They feared him. They did not like the way he had played along with the corrupt Tammany machine in New York—only to lose its votes in the end. Mostly they felt he had exhibited a very disturbing lack of force, or willingness to battle for things, a tendency to compromise. Those who were with him were with him with many reservations.

His subordinates and department heads found him hesitant, evasive, difficult to follow. They never quite knew where he stood, when he was really behind them, when he might step away. There is no doubt that his habit was to seek to please everyone, to court everybody's approval. Every caller went away feeling he had a friend in the governor who was in agreement with him. The stories on this point are well authenticated and innumerable. One well-known reporter, friendly to Roosevelt, wrote: "Those having dealings with him find the effusiveness of his good will a hindrance, for they often leave a meeting with the impression that he is committed to one policy only to find that he advocates its opposite." It is very difficult to find any of those who served under him as governor who do not hold this view.

III

Building the New Deal

As THE DATE for the conventions in 1932 approached, the imperious issue that commanded everyone's attention was the depression. It was apparent that the country had lost faith in Hoover and that it was looking for a new savior. All sorts of men with all sorts of plans, programs and panaceas were contesting for public approval. And Roosevelt was shaping up his own plans for the redemption of the country.

We shall make but little headway toward understanding what followed unless we get a clear idea of the nature of the great collapse and the causes that lay behind it. Those causes are obscured because they are so much mixed up with human and dramatic incidents that were mere excrescences and irritants and aggravations of the depression rather than its real cause. Of course Hoover, being president when it came, was denounced as the author of the disaster. Coolidge, who had had really more to do with it than Hoover, was very little blamed, because he had escaped from the White House before the blow came. But in truth the causes of the depression were wholly unconnected with any man or group of men.

This, after all, is the capitalist system working in a

money economy—a system of private property, private profit, individual enterprise distributing its products and services by means of money. It works according to certain well-known laws. If we do not know quite how to counteract them, we at least do know what they are.

I have already pointed out that long-term private investment is the dynamic element in this system. Men save. They will not spend the money they save except to make money with it. This we call investment. That is, a man will not buy something to eat with his savings. He will buy a machine to make something to eat or sell at a profit. Or he will lend money to someone for that purpose or to build a house or a railroad or a utility. Therefore the savings of the people will never get spent if they do not invest them. Hence investment is the only instrument there is—save taxation—for returning the savings of the people back into the stream of spending.

We have another device for stimulating the capitalist system. It is called credit inflation. It is a method of creating funds for investment over and above those available from savings. When you borrow money from a commercial bank, it does not hand you cash. The bank accepts your note and your collateral and gives you credit on its books for a "deposit." When you make a loan from a bank you actually increase the bank's deposits. The bank creates a deposit by the sheer acting of making a loan to you. If you draw the money out, you do so by means of a check given to someone. That someone usually puts the check in his bank, and the deposit created by your loan is not destroyed but merely transferred from your bank to the bank of the man to whom you gave the check.

In this way immense supplies of bank money are created —really bank deposits or bank debits which can be used for money and are used for money. This is done whenever there is active investment. And when these bank funds are thus increased, they in turn can be used again for further investment.

This is the manner in which credit is made available in the capitalist system—from actual money savings of the people and from bank loans.

An abundant supply of this credit is essential to the functioning of the capitalist system, because without it new enterprises cannot be started and old ones cannot be expanded. Whenever a new enterprise is started or an old one expanded, it is done by putting into it somebody's savings or credit obtained from some bank.

Two things must therefore meet—first, opportunity for investment, second, credit. Men must see what they believe to be opportunities for investing their money, and there must be others—individual savers and banks—with the resources and the willingness to lend.

This is why people speak of the importance of what they call the heavy-goods industries. This is not a good name for it. Investment-goods industries would be a better name for it—those industries in which the buying is done by persons with their savings or their credit, such as the building industry, the railroads, industrial plants, utilities, etc.

The reason we had such a great boom between 1923 and 1929 is the enormous investments that had been made out of savings and bank credit. I have already indicated that it was the automobile and the immense changes made in the face of the country by the automobile, such as the building of suburbs, garages, filling stations, service stations, the gasoline and rubber industries to suppy automobiles and the great system of highways. It involved immense expansion in the utility industry, which was growing at a rapid pace and using up billions every year in credits. It was helped by the moving-picture industry —not the actual moving-picture producers themselves, but the necessity for investing billions in over twenty-six thousand theaters. It was hurried along by the great development in household utilities—vacuum cleaners, washing machines, etc.—that involved the construction of great factories. All of these things were done with funds borrowed from savers or from the banks on mortgages and on securities.

As long as this investment industry was flourishing, we had a boom.

It was obvious that the moment people stopped building, expanding and borrowing investment funds to do these things, the boom would crash, and this, of course, is what happened. Investment stops for various reasons. Generally we may say it stops when people do not want to build or expand any more or when those who have money do not want to lend. The great question in this depression was: why did investment stop? Mr Hoover blamed it on conditions in Europe. Liberal reformers blamed it on Wall Street. Others blamed it on labor. Others said it was due to the drop in farm prices. Slowly more and more people came around to blaming it on Hoover, who, of course, had nothing to do with it.

Men stop building and expanding either when there is no more demand for what they build or produce or no more profit in it. Men stop lending when they cannot see security for their loans. In this depression the trouble started not with the lenders, but with the investors. People and banks were willing to lend long after enterprisers were willing to build and expand. They did continue lending, but they were lending not to builders and expanders and producers but to speculators who had not yet perceived what had happened.

The trouble lay in certain great areas of investment. The investor does not invest his money in some abstract idea of investment but in a particular enterprise. He puts his money in a building, in a railroad, a utility company, a manufacturing plant. The jam had begun in these areas of investment. First, in the building industry, prices had been pushed up. Labor costs had increased and labor practices had become so costly to builders that it was no longer profitable to put money in a building. The cost of production ruined the investment. The reason for this we shall see later. It is one of the most important factors in the whole picture.

Other forces checked the building boom. The building of houses and apartments for low-income groups had long ceased to be profitable and was abandoned. The profits continued in the high-income apartment groups. It was so easy to get money on real-estate bonds for this purpose, and the money was not in operating the buildings but in selling the bonds. Hence high-priced apartment and apartment-hotel buildings and office buildings went up without very much regard to the demand, until the market was glutted with this kind of building.

In the railroad field a whole collection of factors was making further railroad expansion unprofitable. Too many railroads were skating on thin ice. The debts of the railroads were overwhelming. The tremendous competition of bus and truck and private automobile together with certain regulatory elements that remained inflexible choked off railroad building, expansion, modernization and investment.

In the utilities it was somewhat different. The utilities got a black eye from the depredations of audacious and unscrupulous adventurers like Insull. Utility properties were converted into stocks and pumped into the stock markets, pushed up in price by dishonest manipulative practices until there was no longer any profit for the investor.

There were other factors. The country had gone mad on stock-market speculation. Little by little, people with money were unwilling to put the money into productive enterprises and wait for years for their profit. They preferred rather to put their money into Wall Street, buying a share at 50 today and selling it at 75 next month. One result of this was that countless billions of investment funds were racing around Wall Street from one speculator to another, rather than going into producing machinery and buildings. We produced too much of this bank money I have referred to—money created by loans at banks. Billions in loans were made without proper security.

Thus far I have described conditions without any reference, save one (in the utility industry), to the bad and dishonest conditions that had grown up in finance. Even if these conditions had not developed, the whole situation was bad, economically indefensible, and was bound to crack. But unfortunately it was aggravated by a whole set of half-mad, half-dishonest business practices. The most important of these were in the banks. Many banks had fallen into the hands of adventurers instead of bankers. Holding companies bought up the banks, as they bought up utility companies. Bank affiliates were organized to enable the bankers to use the banks' funds in their own adventures. And by thoroughly immoral devices of manipulation the prices of stocks were driven up to incredibly foolish levels and these stocks made the basis of billions in bank loans. When the crack came, therefore, not only did we have an economic slump stemming from the normal functioning of economic law, but we had that slump turned into an unprecedented disaster because of the extent to which the foundations of our whole financial system were weakened by foolish and dishonest practices.

2

This was the problem that confronted the American people as the two great parties met in June 1932 to choose candidates and outline an approach to recovery.

The problem, of course, by this time had become profoundly aggravated. Because the slump itself had brought in its train a multitude of problems. Unemployment was mounting so that by June 1932 there were probably eleven million out of work. The banks had been failing, and failures were increasing at an alarming rate. The farmer, having lost his market in town, was in distress—his products declined in price, he could not meet his mortgage charges and his debt; creditors were knocking at his door. The farmers were in revolt.

Because profits and pay rolls had dwindled, states, cities and the Federal government could not collect enough taxes to meet their operating expenses and were sliding into the red. And this was further aggravated by the demand upon their treasuries for relief. Thus we had what were called unemployment problems, banking problems, farm problems, tax problems. But at the bottom they were all the problems of an economic system that was slowly running down.

The whole problem divided itself into four parts: (1)

How to take care of the victims of the disaster until it was mended. (2) How to correct the economic system—make it function more smoothly and justly in the future. (3) How to correct certain grave social injustices and maladjustments. (4) How to produce recovery.

As the situation developed, a fifth problem presented itself. Those who knew something of the economic system saw it coming with terrifying swiftness. This was the problem of the crisis. That is to say, to many in June and certainly after September it was obvious that the banking system was heading for a complete collapse—a collapse that would paralyze all business until it was corrected and that would intensify, for the time being, all of the other dislocations of the depression.

To sum up all this, the problem was:

1. *Relief*. How to provide the unemployed with food, clothing, shelter until they could be given work.

2. *Economic Reform*. How to correct the system so that the flow of investment would be more nearly continuous and to protect the economic system from exploitation by those whose adventures tended to jam it.

3. *Social Justice*. How the economic system could be made to produce more widespread employment, how the unemployed and the aged and the weak could be provided against the exigencies of occasional unemployment, old age, sickness, oppression, etc.

4. *Recovery*. How to get long-term investment in industrial building and expansion started again.

Roosevelt, facing the coming battle for the nomination, set about, as all candidates do, assembling a collection of solutions for the various problems vexing the nation. And he began, as most candidates do, by gathering about him a group of advisers. Louis Howe, his long-time political secretary, of course was there. But in January 1932 Roosevelt asked Raymond Moley, professor of government at Columbia University, to assist him and later had Moley bring together a group of men who could collaborate in forming a general program. All these men did not come into the picture at the same time. But the group included, besides Moley and Howe, Samuel Rosenman, New York Supreme Court justice and a friend of Roosevelt's; Rexford Tugwell and Lindsay Rogers, Columbia University economics professors; Adolph Berle, Jr, authority on everything under the sun; Ralph Robey, a young economist from New York University whose field was finance. After the nomination the group took in others, including General Hugh Johnson. Together these men proceeded to forge what came to be known as the New Deal. And they were widely advertised as Roosevelt's brain trust. The term "brain trust" was supplied by James Kieran, a correspondent of the New York *Times*. The term "New Deal" was not invented by Roosevelt, but by Moley. Roosevelt, up to this time, although for years in public life, had made no contributions either of phrase, principles or terms to political life. He gained some fame by dubbing Al Smith the "Happy Warrior" in his speech nominating Smith in the convention of 1924. That speech was written for Roosevelt, a number of men working on it. The term "Happy Warrior" was contributed by Judge Proskauer. Roosevelt's famous paragraph in the Farley case proclaiming a code of honesty for public officials was written by Raymond Moley. And now the terms "brain trust" and "New Deal" which he used were originated by two other men.

Indeed, it is interesting here to make a brief inventory of the man who was now about to be made into a great

national figure and hero—to look for an instant at what we might call the raw material with which the publicity men and the public imagination would work in the coming "build-up" of a new public figure. He was fifty years old, six feet one, broad-shouldered, handsome, with that kind of distinguished visage we are accustomed to in actors. He had a good voice. It had not been very successful in platform speaking, but over the radio it had a special quality of clarity and charm. He was crippled, but in the best of health. He had an extraordinarily agreeable manner amounting to charm and an exuberant friendliness that everyone seemed to like. He was a man who had avoided quarrels and controversies, so that he had few enemies. He knew little or nothing of economics, confessed freely his ignorance of taxation, and was quite naïve on the subject of finance. He was not a student, not a reader, not interested in either the mundane or the transcendental sciences. Even Emil Ludwig, in his official biography gotten mostly from Roosevelt himself, observes that Roosevelt was "remote alike from religion and philosophy." He was not a thinker. He was a man of impressions and leanings and sentiments. What he knew he picked up mostly in conversation—a scrap here, a bit there.

He had a number of hobbies. First was his love of his picture collection of battleships and his interest in war vessels, particularly old war vessels and old naval books. He liked to sail a boat. He was deeply interested in the Warm Springs Foundation established for the cure and research of infantile paralysis. He found a great deal of pleasure in his stamp collection. In those moments when other men are apt to turn to a book, Roosevelt will turn to his stamp albums. His knowledge of history, science, philosophy, literature was quite limited. He knew the political history of his time, but it was largely the story of men and personalities rather than of measures and movements. Indeed Roosevelt thinks in terms of personalities. To him a political question is a difference of opinion between two men. He feels he can solve a question by bringing both men together and getting them to shake hands and stop arguing.

He had never done very much writing. He was one of those many public men who were willing to have their speeches written for them. But he was an excellent reader. He was warmhearted, generous in his sympathies, wanted to do something for the underdog. He was vacillating, indecisive, but impulsive. That is, he would put off action or decision on most things until driven to act, but might at any moment, without very much calculation and on the impulse of the instant, rush into some course or movement. He was a good talker in conversation, chatty, pleasant, voluble. This was the man who was soon to be presented to the American people as the great figure to lead it out of the wilderness.

3

Let us now see what he, with the aid of his advisers, fabricated as a program which he called the New Deal.

On the subject of relief he said: "I am opposed to any form of dole. I do not believe that the state has any right merely to hand out money" (p. 43).[1]

"Under no circumstances," he said again, "shall any money be paid in the form of a dole or any other form

[1] The page numbers in parentheses used in this and succeeding paragraphs refer to the pages in Vol. I of *The Public Papers and Addresses of Franklin D. Roosevelt, 1928–1932,* issued by the President and edited by Judge Samuel I. Rosenman.

by the local welfare officer to any unemployed or his family" (p. 463).

He was for relief rather than public works. He wired Senator Robert Wagner in February 1932: "Plans for large public works are possible if the works themselves are carefully planned and economically necessary, but they do not relieve distress at the moment" (p. 468).

On the subject of spending for recovery he said: "People suggest that a huge expenditure of public funds by the Federal government and by state and local governments will completely solve the unemployment problem. . . . Let us admit frankly that it would be only a stopgap" (p. 625).

In July 1932 Roosevelt quoted with approval the Democratic platform promising "a saving of not less than 25 per cent of the cost of the Federal government" (p. 661). He denounced Hoover for not reducing annual expenses to meet decreasing revenues; for pouring "more government money into business" (p. 680). He said: "I accuse the present administration [Hoover's] of being the greatest spending administration in peace times in all our history," and added, "On my part, I ask you [the electorate] very simply *to assign to me* the task of reducing the annual operating expenses of your national government" (p. 761).

While Roosevelt was opposed to heavy government spending, he was even more opposed to government spending of borrowed money. "Revenues," he said, "must cover expenditures by one means or another. Any government, like any family, can for a year spend a little more than it earns, but you and I know that a continuation of that habit means the poorhouse" (p. 663). He said: "High-sounding, newly invented phrases cannot sugar-coat the pill. Let us have the courage to stop borrowing to meet continuing deficits. Stop the deficits" (p. 662).

He was particularly opposed to the government's borrowing at the banks (p. 806). He repeatedly condemned Hoover in the strongest language for permitting deficits. "I regard it as a positive duty," he said, "of the government to raise *by taxes* whatever sums may be necessary to keep them [the unemployed] from starvation" (p. 798).

At Pittsburgh, in a speech on the budget, he said, after working up with great dramatic effect to the point: "Now I am going to give you good people a real shock. Instead of the government running into the red for those two years to the tune of $150,000,000, the deficit on June 30, 1932, was for the two fiscal years three and three quarter billion dollars" (p. 801). Again he said: "If the present rate on that budget [Hoover's] continues, the true deficit as of June 30 next year will be over $1,600,000,000—a deficit so great that it makes you catch your breath" (p. 805). There is no point in multiplying these quotations.

On the subject of government and business he said: "I share the President's [Hoover's] complaint against regimentation, but, unlike him, I dislike it not only when it is carried on by an informal group, an unofficial group amounting to an economic government of the United States, *but also when it is done by the government of the United States itself*" (p. 680). He denounced the Republican leaders for "fostering regimentation without stint or limit." He said in a radio address in March 1930: "The doctrine of regulation and legislation by 'master minds' in whose judgment and will all the people may gladly and quietly acquiesce has been too glaringly apparent at Washington these last ten years. Were it possible to find master minds so unselfish, so willing to decide unhesitat-

ingly against their own personal interests or private preju-
dices, men almost God-like in their ability to hold the
scales of justice with an even hand, such a government
might be in the interest of the country. But there are none
such on our political horizon, and we cannot expect a
complete reversal of all the teachings of history" (p. 571).

He adopted the traditional Democratic position against
"the tendency to concentrate power at the top of a government structure alien to our system" (p. 96). He put great
emphasis on the subject of states' rights (p. 570) and made
a special point of the "sacred, time-honored American
principle of the separation of the judicial, legislative and
executive departments of the government" (p. 348).

On the question of the farmers Roosevelt denounced
the Republicans for having destroyed the foreign markets
for the farmers' surplus production by means of the
Fordney-McCumber and Grundy tariffs. He denounced
the whole Republican approach to farm rehabilitation and
particularly called for the "immediate repeal of those pro-
visions of law that compel the Federal government to go
into the markets to purchase, to sell, to speculate in farm
products in a futile attempt to reduce farm surpluses."
He poured out his scorn upon Hoover's secretary of agriculture *who invented the cruel joke of calling on the
farmers to allow 20 per cent of their wheat lands to lie
idle, to plow up every third row of cotton and shoot every
tenth cow*" (p. 79).

He suggested a plan and insisted that it would be a
plan that "does not cost the government any money." He
also said he favored concentrating this work in the Department of Agriculture, and he demanded economies there,
pointing out that it was filled with useless jobs, and promised to cut away its useless functions and jobs. Only exist-

ing agencies, he said, should be used, and as far as possible the work should be done by local bodies.

Then he outlined his plan. He declared there must be national planning in agriculture, which meant a planned use of the land to make the best use of our soil, a reduction and more equitable distribution of taxes and an effort to get local bodies to reduce the tax burden, to refinance farm mortgages by reducing interest. Finally, the great objective was to cut the difference between industrial prices and farm prices, between the price the farmer pays for what he buys and the price he gets for what he sells. To do this, his plan was to pay cash benefits to farmers who raised surplus crops in order to offset the tariff on the things they bought. In return for this the farmers should be willing not to increase their production. This should all be voluntary, *must be financed by the farmers themselves*—as far as possible through co-operatives. It must cost the government nothing.

As to unemployment, of course his remedy was that unemployment should be reduced by recovery, and the thing that was holding back recovery was the high tariffs and the government deficits. By wiping out the government deficits and reducing the tariffs, recovery would be insured. But for those unemployed he favored the use of certain types of public works as a further emergency means of stimulating employment and the issuance of bonds to pay for such public works, "but I have pointed out that no economic end is served if we merely build without building for a necessary purpose. Such works of course should in so far as possible be self-sustaining if they are to be financed by the issuing of bonds."

And then Governor Roosevelt, in his speech accepting the nomination, revealed his great plan for employing a million men. He said: "There are tens of millions of acres east of the Mississippi in abandoned farms, cut-over lands now growing up in worthless brush. . . . We face a future of soil erosion and timber famine. It is clear that economic foresight and immediate employment march hand in hand in the call for the reforestation of these vast areas. In so doing *employment can be given to a million men.* That is the kind of public work that is self-sustaining and therefore capable of being financed by the issuance of bonds which are made secure by the fact that the growth of tremendous crops will provide adequate security for the investment. Yes, I have a very definite program for providing employment by that means. I have done it and I am doing it today in the State of New York." But this was to be paid for out of unexpended money in the Treasury—no taxes, no borrowing.

In the case of the railroads he denounced Hoover's suggestion of "further credits to the railroads, thus obviously increasing their debt and fixed charges. This policy, my friends, may put off the evil day for a short period, but standing alone and by itself it makes the day of reckoning more tragic for the nation when it comes" (p. 722).

His plan, he said, was to take the railroads out of the red, put them on their feet and *reduce their debts instead of increasing them.* As a part of this he advocated a revised receivership procedure, consolidation of the roads, regulation of railroad holding companies, regulation by the Interstate Commerce Commission of competing modes of transportation and changing the policy of enforced competition between the railroads.

One of the great and important parts of his whole New Deal was his utility or power program. He announced that he was against government ownership, but that if cities wished to turn to government ownership they should have the opportunity to do so as a rod over the heads of the private utilities. He favored the ownership and development of the Federal and state power resources (water power) by the states and the Federal government, with private distribution. But the government should have the right if necessary to force better rates, to go into distribution, thus "holding a birch rod in the cupboard." He referred to Muscle Shoals and Boulder Dam (the latter was already being developed by the Federal government), to the St Lawrence River and the Columbia River as proper places for development.

Thus we may summarize the program that Governor Roosevelt offered to the people as his New Deal as follows:

That he would put an end to government spending and above all to government deficits, particularly government borrowing from the banks; and would revise and reform the tariff. These two things were the chief obstacles to recovery.

That he would adopt an allotment plan for the farmers, but that this would cost the government no money, would be self-sustaining, would be centralized in the Department of Agriculture, no new agencies would be created—on the contrary, the Department of Agriculture would be subjected to great economies by the reduction of its functions and its personnel.

That he would put an end to government support of the excessive railroad debts and would force the railroads to scale down their indebtedness.

That in the domain of power he would recognize the permanence of private capital and ownership as against public ownership as the normal mode of operating utilities, but favored government development of water-power sites by states and the Federal government, which was Al Smith's plan. He added to this, however, that while he favored private distribution, the government reserved the right to step in to force equitable rates—to provide a yard-stick.

That on the matter of relief he was opposed to a dole and on the question of spending for recovery he opposed that as a stopgap but was willing to issue bonds for public works that were self-sustaining—which was only another way of saying he believed in what Hoover believed in: self-liquidating projects.

He declared himself against all forms of regimentation, regimentation by powerful individuals and "by the government of the United States itself," and, above all, all regulation and legislation by "master minds." He denounced monopoly, the merger of competitive business into monopolies, and demanded a strict and impartial enforcement of the anti-trust laws. He was against the concentration of power in the Federal government, was for the protection of states' rights and "the sacred and time-honored American principle of the separation of the judicial, legislative and executive departments."

4

This was quite a different New Deal from the one that emerged after the inauguration. The statements Roosevelt made before the election make curious reading when placed alongside of the actual performances and the statements made after he took office. The strange contradictions are not easily resolved. One wonders which of these New Deals—the one outlined in the campaign or the one put into effect after March 4, 1933—conforms more closely to Roosevelt's own philosophy. How far did he subscribe to the plans he proclaimed while governor and how far does he subscribe to the measures he urged after he came to power? Where does the real Roosevelt lie?

It is not easy to answer. There are some explanations of the many and vital contradictions. It is a fact that you can find statements from Roosevelt's speeches on almost every side of every public question. This may be explained by the fact that most of his important speeches are written for him by someone else. It is a bad habit for a public man to follow. He is sure to find himself uttering sentiments one day which will be very different some future day when the speech is written by some different author. Roosevelt has his speeches written for him because writing a good speech is not one of his own talents. Of course occasionally he does write a speech—usually a short one. And it is possible invariably to tell when he does the job. His style is quite discoverable.

Indeed, it is a very interesting diversion to trace the various styles which appear in his speeches. Almost any student of composition—any experienced copyreader— would be able to divide his speeches according to their authors. I do not mean he could name the authors, but he could say this batch was written by one man and this batch by another, and so on, ending with a small batch written by the President himself.

Many of the President's speeches while governor and in the campaign were written in a strikingly finished style. So much was this true that newspapers began to comment upon our "stylist" President. They could not have known, of course, that the speeches were not written by the President any more than the speeches uttered by an actor on the stage are the product of his pen. It would be as proper to praise Mr Walter Hampden for his magnificent poetic gifts because of the noble verses he utters in *Hamlet*. The authorship of many of the speeches is now known. Many of the campaign speeches were written by Moley, one or two by Hugh Johnson. Berle wrote some and had a hand in others. Ernest Lindley wrote the Oglethorpe speech. Moley wrote the speech of acceptance. Louis Howe wrote some. After the election, speeches were written by other composers—which accounts for many of the sentiments hostile to the campaign speeches. Once in a while Roosevelt himself dictates one. The famous Madison Square Garden speech in the second campaign, which drew so much praise, was written by Tommy Corcoran.

The noble first inaugural was the product of several minds. Roosevelt himself contributed little or nothing. He was the actor who read it. Roosevelt's attitude toward speechmaking and toward economic policies is well illustrated in two cases.

A speech on the tariff had to be prepared. Moley asked Senator Cordell Hull to draft a speech based on his ideas. The Hull speech when put in Moley's hands was an outright old-fashioned "down with the tariff" oration. Feeling that such a speech would be impossible, Moley asked General Hugh Johnson to prepare an alternate draft. Hull called for a flat cut of all tariffs by at least 10 per cent. The Johnson draft called for gradual reopening of the channels of commerce by skillful bilateral negotiation. The speeches were wholly different, different in their approach and their philosophy. Moley showed both drafts to Roosevelt.

Roosevelt read them over, handed them back to Moley and said: "Weave the two together"—no comment on the economic contents, no opinions on the contradictory views or which one should prevail, just "weave the two to-gether."[1]

Even more extraordinary is the story of the acceptance speech at Chicago before the Democratic convention. It had been decided that in the event of Roosevelt's nomination he would fly to Chicago and deliver his acceptance speech there. Moley wrote the speech and left it in Albany with Roosevelt and Sam Rosenman. It remained as written but slightly reduced. The last five paragraphs were added. Whether these five paragraphs were written by Roosevelt or Rosenman, it is difficult to say. They do not have on them the marks of Roosevelt's style, save in the last two paragraphs. They were probably written by Roosevelt and revised by Rosenman. Otherwise the speech was as written by Moley.

Moley went to the convention. He was told to get Louis Howe's approval of this speech. But Howe, thinking Rosenman had written it and cordially disliking Rosenman, refused to approve it. Instead Howe wrote a whole new speech himself.

Roosevelt was nominated and left by airplane from Hyde Park for Chicago. Louis Howe and Moley both were at the Chicago airport when Roosevelt arrived. Howe, by reason of his old intimacy with Roosevelt, got into the motorcar with him. He told Roosevelt of his speech and undertook to get Roosevelt to deliver it without even reading it. This story is related by Moley, who, next to Howe, was the closest man to Roosevelt. Had it not come from so authoritative a source it would be almost incredible. No man knew Roosevelt so well as Louis Howe, and this incident means that Howe knew Roosevelt well enough to believe that he could get him to deliver a speech accept-

[1] *After Seven Years*, by Raymond Moley.

ing the nomination for the presidency of the United States without even reading it. Howe handed the speech to Roosevelt on the platform as he was being introduced to the convention. Roosevelt had in his hand the Moley speech and the Howe speech. It was a difficult moment for him. Which should he deliver? He had read and corrected the Moley speech. He had not even seen the Howe speech. He was about to accept a call to lead the Democratic party with that speech. He did a thoroughly characteristic Roosevelt thing. He began to read. Moley, sitting in the convention, was horrified to hear strange sentences that were not in the speech he had written. Roosevelt was reading the Howe speech. Having read almost the whole of its first page, he then went on with the Moley speech.

From all this we may begin to form a fairly definite picture of the man who became President of the United States and upon whose mind poured all the difficult problems of meeting one of the great economic crises in our history. One thing stands out with striking clarity—that in a great economic crisis there came to leadership a man who was never in the slightest degree interested in economic problems, had no understanding of them and who in a grave financial crisis had no interest in or understanding of the problems of finance. It helps us to understand why at a later period he could propose building fifty thousand airplanes that would cost seven billion dollars and say to the country that the means of raising the money was a minor detail.

IV

The Crisis

IN WHAT FOLLOWS HERE there will be no point in pursuing the events of the next seven years in chronological order. It will add to clarity if we follow them according to the phases and topics as they develop.

As Roosevelt came into power, the crisis intervened—a kind of disordered and hectic interlude that had to be dealt with before either he or Congress could turn to the problems of reform or recovery.

There is a kind of assumption that this crisis had nullified all the thinking and planning that had gone before, that it in some way changed the problem and confronted the government with a wholly different economic scene. That, of course, is not in any sense true.

The mismanagement, the exploitations, the dishonesties that had marked American banking for over a decade were now bringing their harvest—most of the banks were ruined, the depositors were standing in long lines for their money, the very motor of the economic system was being stalled. President Hoover, a year before, had attempted to save the inevitable banking disaster by the establishment of the Reconstruction Finance Corporation, to put Federal funds behind the tottering banks. It could not save them. Already in December the inevitable debacle was in sight. In the brief interlude between the election and the inauguration, before the new President came to power and the old President had for all practical purposes lost power, the situation got out of hand. The forces of crisis were hurried, and as Roosevelt was sworn in, one half of the banks of the country were ripe for collapse and fifteen or sixteen million people were out of work.

Almost the first act of the President was to close all of the banks in order to prevent all of the banks from closing by themselves. The next duty was to sort out the sheep from the goats, the good banks from the bad ones, to keep the bad ones closed and to put the government's credit behind the reopened banks in such a way as to keep them open.

Roosevelt closed the banks, which was the proper and inescapable thing to do. Hoover had already prepared to do this, and the orders issued by the new President for the closing of the banks were in no sense different from those that had been prepared by Ogden Mills, Hoover's secretary of the treasury, for the same purpose. There was literally no choice of courses here. The only choice was in how the banks should be reopened. The terms and conditions of that were worked out in the Treasury Department in collaboration between William Woodin, the new secretary of the treasury, and the officials of the Hoover administration who remained to assist. It was at this point that certain extreme progressive and radical supporters of the President felt the government should have taken over the banks. It is entirely probable that such an idea never entered Roosevelt's mind, and it is wholly fortunate that it did not.

On the whole the banking crisis was well managed. When it was managed and the banks reopened, the economic problem presented was essentially precisely the one that the country had been facing for a year. The inevitable economic disintegration had merely progressed further. The necessity for action had merely become more imperative.

What had changed, however, was the temper and the mood of the people. Doing something about the economic system and its attendant social problems had become enormously easier because resistance had been broken by events. The country had become chastened. There was a revealing and humiliating consciousness of the sins of the old decade. The great and once arrogant financial and industrial chieftains were thoroughly discredited. Some of them were in disgrace, others actually in flight, many of them trembling lest the whole economic system should come down about their ears. There was literally no opposition to doing now what had to be done. An excellent example of this is to be found in the very subject of government spending. Hoover had attempted a little spending on a small scale. The whole Democratic organization, with Governor Roosevelt leading the pack, denounced him for his extravagance. If spending and borrowing were the way out and Hoover had attempted it, he would have been crucified. But it was now possible for Roosevelt, who had been the leading critic of spending, to pour out billions. This was because the people as a whole had finally been forced to abandon the illusion that prosperity was around the corner.

In other words, the immensity of the disaster had, without changing the problem, opened the road for the new President to do almost anything he chose to do.

V

The New Deal—Second Edition

BEFORE IT IS POSSIBLE to understand what happened now, it is necessary to take note of two powerful influences in public thinking. One was quite new; the other, quite old.

The first was the movement for what was being called a planned society. It originated with men who were either devoted to the socialist theory of economic organization or were strongly influenced by it. It was based upon the assumption that society had permitted itself to become the helpless and unresisting victim of economic forces and laws; that our country possessed unrivaled resources for supplying almost all our needs; that we had the technological skills, the raw materials and a people capable of using these to give abundance to all; that we did not have abundance because we did not sit down together and consider the means by which abundance might be produced. We permitted individuals to run riot in pursuit of their individual objectives. We allowed groups to organize to press for their special interests. No authority gave thought to how much food, how much clothes, how much shelter a nation of 130 million people needed and how that population could organize to produce it. Nor was there any authority to carry out a plan even if one could be contrived.

To this kind of reasoning there is of course no answer. It was simply a question of what kind of plan should be undertaken, who should do the planning and for what purpose. Since there was no notion in anybody's mind in authority of abandoning the capitalist money economy, with its private property and private profit and private enterprise, the problem was obviously how to plan for a system of private property, and this involved an examination of the anatomy of such a system. Whatever plans were made would have to be plans for a democratic society operating a capitalist economy and would have to be, therefore, in harmony with the peculiar genius of such a system. As it was a system of free individuals, such planning would involve searching out the motor powers, the special centers of energy in such a system and taking measures to make them function; to find, as it were, the glands and to provide for their healthy operation neither below nor in excess of normal. The central thesis of these men was that we did not produce enough to provide the good life for all. The central objective was to use our resources and machinery to produce abundance.

Unfortunately many of those who played with this idea got the notion that planning in a capitalist system could be achieved like planning in a collectivist system, where blueprints for industry in the future could be made and laws and rules and regulations governing the behavior of individuals could be set up, with controls on prices, production, the organization of industry. What they overlooked was that the planning authority could not compel individuals to invest their money, could not enforce investment which is the dynamic function in the capitalist system.

Into Washington on the wave of the crisis there swarmed a large group of earnest men, apostles of this school of the planned society. A few of them were men who had thought about this seriously for a long time. Most of them were new converts, half baked, many fresh from Wall Street law and brokerage offices, thrust from their old careers by the disaster, new and almost fanatical followers of the planners.

The other movement was akin to this, yet wholly different. As the planning movement stemmed from the Left, this movement had its origin on the Right. For many years businessmen were afflicted by what they called over-production. In almost every industry enterprisers were producing more goods than they could sell. This has always been true in our present economic system, but it became more serious as our resources increased and the physical machinery and financial credit for utilizing them were perfected. As far back as 1870 in the oil regions of Pennsylvania the producers found that they could pump more oil than they could sell. This brought prices down. They therefore decided that the remedy was to produce less oil and keep prices up. It is entirely possible that this conviction has been the most potent single principle of action in American economic society during the last seventy years. It is a very natural thing for a man in business to feel that he would be more prosperous if there were not so many in competition with him. It is easy to understand that the average manufacturer will think that he can get a better price and hence make a larger profit if he can introduce a little scarcity into his production.

The first means of attaining this objective was through trade associations. They were organized to bring together producers in the same industry to reduce production and to keep up prices and to make it more difficult for others to come into the industry and hence to compete with them. The idea spread to every trade—even to labor unions that sought to limit apprenticeships so as to check the flow of new recruits into their trades.

The next phase of this was through industrial combinations and corporate monopolies. Rockefeller tried the trade association but found that it did not work efficiently to limit production. He then formed a combination between himself and his competitors in a corporation, twelve or fourteen competitors uniting in a single industrial unit. Later the holding company was invented to facilitate this same process. Always it was the effort of producers to control production, to limit it in order to keep up prices, to produce scarcity in the interest of higher prices and profits.

It is useless to quarrel with this. Apparently it is in the very order of human nature that men moved by self-interest will act this way.

The Sherman anti-trust law was adopted in 1890 to check this very thing. Later, under Woodrow Wilson, the Clayton Act and the Federal Trade Commission law were passed to strengthen the government in checking this movement. Men like Woodrow Wilson—who, unlike Roosevelt, was widely read in the history of civilization—realized that this movement, however natural amongst businessmen, was based upon the theory that scarcity in production was essential to high prices and profits.

After the World War this movement, which up to then had been looked upon as lawless, began to put on the vestments of respectability. The Chamber of Commerce of the United States and various trade associations began a movement for what they called "self-rule in industry." The objective was to weaken the enforcement of the anti-trust laws, to change those laws, to modify them, to suspend them in order to enable business groups to get together to adopt codes of ethics, as they said, to outlaw unfair trade practices. Unfair trade practices would include many things that every decent businessman would condemn, such as commercial bribery and false advertising. But they were also made to include such things as the enterpriser's right to produce and to price his goods as he saw fit; to include, indeed, a man's right to expand his business or go into a new business. In other words, under the guise of regulating fairness in competition, powerful business groups wished to get rid of the Sherman and other anti-trust laws in order to confer upon their organized groups the right to make laws for their industries. The conviction had taken root that the economic system must be governed, that the people to govern it were the producers themselves, which meant the employers; that they should govern it through trade associations, that the laws of the United States should be changed to permit this and that the government should authorize it with a kind of general supervision by the government itself.

The central thesis of these men was that we produced too much and that this abundance ruined prices, and their central objective was to keep production down.

To a mind unaccustomed to thinking about these things it was easy to confuse the objectives of the planners with the objectives of the self-rule-in-industry groups. And one of the most amazing spectacles in our history is the manner in which, in those first days of the New Deal, the apostles of planning for abundance and the protagonists of planning for scarcity united under Roosevelt to produce the NRA. The NRA was called planning. The planners of all sorts hailed it—the Chamber of Commerce and the Left Wingers, the champions of abundance and the champions of scarcity.

It was possible only because Franklin D. Roosevelt himself had never thought about these things. It is almost beyond belief that a man so completely oblivious of the powerful and hostile forces at work in his administration and so unaware of what he was doing in a field of economic activity wholly new to him should be hailed by the populace as one of the great leaders of our time.

2

The actual business of putting together the NRA began in March 1933. As it emerged it appeared before the people as a great liberal revolution, the dawn of a new day, under the auspices of liberals, for the people and for labor—and as part of the great forward surge toward abundance. But one must look beyond the throb and pother of those feverish days to understand the swift succession of moves and the cast of characters behind them.

In 1925 the Trade Relations Committee of the Chamber of Commerce of the United States was formed to foster trade practice conferences. Under its sponsorship trade associations adopted codes of practice (President Roosevelt imagined in 1933 that he had originated codes). Price fixing and limiting production were banned in these codes. When President Hoover was elected he promptly put an end to these codes—there were over forty of them. Hoover said that while the codes seemed innocent enough, the officers of the codes, under protection of the codes, sanctioned price and production agreements.

Then came the crash of 1929. In February 1931 the Chamber named a Committee on Continuity of Business and Employment with H. I. Harriman as chairman. That committee reported that *"A freedom of action which might have been justified in the relatively simple life of the last century cannot be tolerated today. . . . We have left the period of extreme individualism."* In other words, the Chamber was all for introducing a little regimentation into our diet. It proposed: (1) Control of production. (2) Modification of the Sherman anti-trust law to permit business units to enter production agreements under government control. (3) A National Economic Council. (4) Unemployment insurance, old-age pensions, government unemployment exchanges. (5) Shorter hours in industry. That was the Chamber of Commerce talking.

About the same time the Committee on Work Periods in Industry, Mr W. P. Litchfield (Goodyear Rubber Company), chairman, reported in the summer of 1932 on its Share-the-Work movement. This committee reported that employers ought to be permitted to unite to agree on shorter hours and minimum wages.

Thus the movement to suspend the Sherman anti-trust law to permit business to organize into units under codes to control production, fix prices, limit competition, govern wage and hour standards, originated with the Chamber of Commerce and business itself. The public imagined that this was a product of the Brain Trust. The Brain Trust was supposed to be a group of young professors, equipped with oversized brainpans—experts in economics, law and government—symbolizing, above all, a break with the

Coolidgian and Hooverian past and its bookless, nescient businessmen. But the idea was an idea of certain businessmen. And the thing they wanted to do was to cut down production to keep up prices—to produce scarcity in the interest of higher prices and profits.

Senator Wagner had a bill for RFC loans for self-liquidating projects. Roosevelt suggested that he have a conference of persons interested. The conference was held in Wagner's office. It included an odd assortment—Meyer Jacobstein; Virgil Jordan, then with the McGraw-Hill business papers; Congressman Clyde Kelly; Harold Moulton (Brookings Institute); Fred I. Kent, vice-president of the Guaranty Trust Company; David Podell, New York trade-association lawyer; Simon Rifkind, Wagner's secretary, Colonel Rorty; Jett Lauck, of the railroad brotherhoods; and James Rand (Remington-Rand Company)—a motley group but not red. This group was full of plans. Kent wanted guarantee of profits; Moulton and Jacobstein were for credits to business; Wagner wanted public works; Podell was for modification of the anti-trust laws. A committee, however, was named to draw a tentative bill. It did. I have seen that bill, and it contains the germ of everything, save the licensing clause, that appeared in the final NRA Act.

All this time another group was at work. Jerome Frank and others were interested in national planning along the George Soule idea—planning for abundance. John Dickinson, Wall Street lawyer, then assistant secretary of commerce and attorney for the Sugar Trust, had a series of proposals closely paralleling the Chamber of Commerce plans. Dickinson and Frank somehow got together, and thereafter the preparation of an acceptable bill was carried on by them along with Podell and Rifkind.

At the same time General Hugh Johnson was at work in Moley's office on a plan to organize business. He wrote a short bill containing an outright grant of power to the President to organize industry to give trade associations authority to regulate competition, prices, production, wages, hours. A day or two later he joined the Wagner group. Donald Richberg came in a little later. After that, little by little, Johnson and Richberg, supported by the President, took over the final drafting of a bill.

What they produced was a plan for self-rule in industry by trade associations under supervision of a government bureau called the National Recovery Administration—the NRA. It specifically suspended the anti-trust laws, thus successfully completing a war that business had waged for fifty years. It was the one thing that appealed most strongly to Roosevelt's imagination. He imagined he had been the instrument of creating a revolution in American industry. This was his idea of a planned economy. It was a plan for organizing each industry under a code. The code was to be drawn by the industry and submitted to the NRA, of which General Johnson became the head. Labor and consumers had nothing to do with drawing the codes. They could appear before the administrator and object to any part of a code before it was approved, but the codes were drawn by the employer associations. Donald Richberg later said that the trade associations were asked to Washington and told to write their own tickets. They most certainly did.

For instance, the Steel Code was drawn by the representatives of the American Iron and Steel Institute, and it set up the Institute as the code authority. Thus it went throughout the field of industry—some seven hundred codes drawn up by the employers with a code authority representing them, usually their trade association, making thousands of rules and regulations with the force of law, binding upon them and the people of the United States.

This was one of the most amazing spectacles of our times, and represented probably the gravest attack upon the whole principle of the democratic society in our political history. The theory of our government is that laws are to be enacted only by the representatives of the people chosen by them. When a group of men, however chosen, sit down to make rules fixing prices, controlling production, setting out the conditions of competition, defining the conditions upon which a man may enter a business, fixing the amount of floor space or machinery he will have, they are enacting laws, by whatever name they are called, particularly when they are enforceable by the public authorities and in many cases with jail sentences. These laws were being enacted not by Congress or a legislature or a board of aldermen or a public official of any kind, but by a group of men called a code authority, elected in most cases by the employers in their respective industries. Under this plan a group of employers, elected by other employers, could sit around a table—like a legislature—and enact laws binding on the community. Anyone who violated them could be put in jail. Not only did they enact the laws, but they united in themselves the executive power to enforce compliance, vested with police power.

Perhaps this is a good plan. Perhaps this is the way society ought to be managed. But it is not the democratic way. The country was divided into provinces—economic provinces as distinguished from geographical provinces. The geographical provinces—the states and counties—continued to be run on the democratic plan by popularly elected legislators and executives. The economic provinces

—the province of steel, of textiles, of millinery, etc.—were run by legislators and police (compliance officers) elected not by the people in the industries on the democratic principle but by a handful of employers. And if this system had continued in force and our development had progressed along that line, we would have continued to move further and further from the democratic plan and in the direction of the corporate state of Mr Mussolini. For this was the beginning of the corporate state, only we called the corporatives codes.

This whole plan was declared unconstitutional by the Supreme Court of the United States—not by a five-to-four decision, but unanimously. Men like Justice Cardozo, Brandeis and Stone joined vigorously in the decision. The reason given was that the NRA was *an abdication by Congress of its constitutional powers to make laws* governing our economic society.

The strangest feature of this episode was that this serious blow to our democracy was carried on to the cheers of many of the so-called liberals who flocked to Washington to support the New Deal. Around the country generally many sincere liberals and progressives were completely confused by the whole performance. Everything that was done was done in an atmosphere of hectic excitement and with speeches and declarations and proclamations couched in the language of liberalism. The planning for scarcity was carried on with the language of the planning for abundance.

At the same time the whole project was given the appearance of being a great charter of liberty for labor. Labor had nothing to do with making the codes—had merely the power of protest that any citizen had. But the law recognized in labor the right of collective bargaining.

As a matter of fact, as it turned out this was a delusion because it merely gave to labor what it already had, namely, the right of collective bargaining provided it could force it on the employers. And what actually happened was that a few powerful unions under strong leadership, like the coal, Ladies' Garment Workers, Amalgamated Clothing Workers under Lewis, Hillman and Dubinsky, did get a great deal because of their numerical and financial strength and their vigorous leadership and their militant tactics. The great victories of the CIO in the steel, automobile and other industries were won after the NRA had passed out of existence.

But while the NRA was formally killed by the Supreme Court, it was riding swiftly to its doom through the sheer confusion and folly of its organization. General Johnson, the first administrator, had resigned, and after a brief interval in which Donald Richberg headed it, the NRA was led by Mr S. Clay Williams. Mr Williams was and is the head of the Reynolds Tobacco Company. He went to Washington when the NRA was formed to protect the great tobacco companies, fought labor in the NRA, declared vehemently that he would fight the NRA to the Supreme Court if necessary on any effort to give labor any rights, and ended by being *appointed by President Roosevelt the administrator of the NRA.*

As for Mr Richberg, who became then a sort of assistant president, he presently left the administration to become one of the most excessively employed lawyers in Washington—representing oil companies, motor companies, Latin-American dictators, the Transamerica Corporation, while at the same time maintaining the most intimate relations with the White House.

Incidentally many of the administrators of the NRA,

the AAA, the SEC and other government bodies are now busily engaged as attorneys for the big business interests with which they were in contact while they served the government.

The NRA as a chapter in political government becomes plain only when you understand the man who made it possible—President Roosevelt. The man who had denounced Hoover for regimentation, who attacked the Republicans for not enforcing the anti-trust laws, who had proclaimed his devotion to freedom of enterprise and to the traditions of democracy, without retracting any of these bold declarations or making any explanation proceeded to put into effect a policy that was the negative of all these things. While at the same time proclaiming his devotion to democracy, he adopted a plan borrowed from the corporative state of Italy and sold it to all the liberals as a great liberal revolutionary triumph. And, curiously, every American liberal who had fought monopoly, who had demanded the enforcement of the anti-trust laws, who had denied the right of organized business groups, combinations and trade associations to rule our economic life, was branded as a tory and a reactionary if he continued to believe these things.

Indeed it is very difficult to explain the strange complacence of the various liberal groups in the presence of the President's surrender to some of the worst elements in that so-called Big Business that they had so mercilessly attacked. The Treasury Department was headed by a Wall Street industrialist while his undersecretary was a member of the most active Washington lobbyist law firm, his assistant secretary a vice-president of the American Bankers Association. The secretary of commerce was a reactionary politician who had been practicing law in

Washington as an income-tax lawyer ever since he left the Internal Revenue Bureau at the time of Woodrow Wilson, while his assistant secretary was an ally of one of the most powerful law firms in Wall Street and at the time represented the Sugar Trust in an attack on the Sherman anti-trust law. One of the first acts of the administration was to organize in the Department of Commerce what was called the Business Advisory Council. It contained the names of some of the biggest businessmen in America. Its objective was, as the secretary of commerce stated publicly, to "weave the pattern for the future economic life of the nation." At a later date when Mr Roosevelt brought his friend, Mr Henry Morgenthau, Jr, a shockingly inexperienced person, in as secretary of the treasury, he named as the Treasury's fiscal adviser Earle Bailie, dominating partner in the firm of J. & W. Seligman & Company, whose then most recent claim to public notice was Senator Hiram Johnson's merciless exposure of his methods in South American financing.

The President was incessantly busy conferring appointments, authority, honors on leading reactionary and conservative figures one week and then passing out appointments, orders and endorsing measures for the Left Wingers the next week. If he approved an act to regulate the stock exchanges (the SEC) to please the liberal and progressive groups, he appointed a Wall Street speculator, Mr Joseph Kennedy, as the head of the commission and literally paralyzed its functions to please the conservative groups. As it happened the conservative groups were more sapient, more experienced apparently and more realistic than the liberal groups. They were quick to see that the President was kidding them a little. But whatever the liberals and conservatives thought about it, the final result was that the President literally got nothing important done.

3

We need not linger on the President's farm policies. Generally they were based on the same principle of scarcity as the NRA. He had promised the voters a farm policy free from such "cruel jokes" as plowing up cotton, not planting wheat, buying up crops to raise prices. His plan would not cost the government a dollar. Now he put into effect the precise reverse of all these policies, all these promises. Instead of asking farmers to plow up or not to plant, he paid them huge sums to do these things. Checks to certain large sugar planters not to plant sugar were as much as a million dollars apiece. The government checks rained on the farms like autumn leaves. He sent agents all over the country—and still does—buying up not only corn and wheat and tobacco and cotton but almost everything under the sun: sweet potatoes in Virginia, oranges in Florida, grapes in New York, apples in the Northwest, eggs everywhere, applesauce in Montana, scores of crops. From March 1933 to December 31, 1935, the government paid out in rental and benefit payments alone $1,108,000,000.

This original farm program came nearer to shocking the mind of the people than any other New Deal adventure. Even Secretary Wallace was a little horrified. "I confess," he said, "I have always had mingled feelings about this plow-up campaign. . . . *To have to destroy a growing crop is a shocking commentary on our civilization.*" It was not a shocking commentary on our civilization. It was a shocking commentary on the man who did it.

The great problem was not how to produce abundance. We know how to do that and have all the machinery for it. The great problem was how to get this abundance to the people. It is a difficult problem—every fair-minded man must admit that. Perhaps we do not know how to do it. But certainly the way to do it is not by destroying the abundance we have. The killing of little pigs, the plowing under of cotton, the wiping out of wheat fields in a nation where fifteen million people were without food and clothing was a spectacle that will long endure as the ultimate in human folly.

The President had subscribed completely to the reactionary theory that the way to produce prosperity is to raise prices. This notion, however little the President knew of economics, was a hangover of an experience he had had as the president of the American Construction Council, an organization of the building industry which as an industry has for years exhausted the devices of combination to get around the Sherman anti-trust laws and keep prices up, competition strangled by trade agreements to limit production and raise prices. The building industry did it so successfully that it practically put an end to the building industry. Roosevelt had served as the head of one of these combinations, and that foggy notion was heavily infused in his thinking.

He kept clamoring for higher prices. He fixed on the price level of 1926 as the norm of prices and declared he wanted to get prices up to that point. He proceeded to do precisely what Hoover had done and what he had denounced. Despite the melancholy lesson of the Hoover Farm Board, the British rubber control, the Brazilian coffee valorization plan, the international sugar agreement and innumerable national and international production-control devices, he began by one device or another to take over the unsalable surpluses of the farmers. Today the surpluses are 13,000,000 bales of cotton and 450,000,000 bushels of wheat.

Outlining his farm plan in that triumphant acceptance speech at Chicago, he concluded, with that staccato emphasis now so well known: "Such a plan as that, my friends, does not cost the government any money."

The President has spent on his farm plans to date $5,828,000,000.

In this year—seven years after its start—he has spent over and above the ordinary costs of the department, $1,328,000,000.

4

It is a melancholy fact, belonging amid the curios of economic history, that in June 1933 the sponsors of this *new* New Deal supposed that a miracle had been worked. Men were put back to work by the NRA industries. Capital and labor were cheering the amazing man who was leading the nation out of chaos back to recovery so swiftly. The stock market was soaring again. The President had a vote of $3,300,000,000 for public works. He was not using it. They told me in Washington it would not be necessary. Then suddenly the stock market, after a three-months' boomlet, crashed. Men were being laid off, prices ceased to rise, the great vessel quivered. At this point two things happened. The President decided to spend, and he launched his money plan.

The money plan is perhaps as perfect an example of how the President's mind works as any in his record. The subject of money was one he understood even less than taxes, which he confessed not to understand. It is an abstruse question calling for years of study and research. Only a few months before he had offered the Treasury portfolio to Carter Glass, unrelenting foe of unorthodox money schemes. This was his gesture of assurance to the sound-money people who feared inflation. Later he forced the amendment of the Thomas inflationary amendment, changing it from an outright direction to inflate to a grant of power to the President—a grant he would never use. It was his way of heading off the inflationists. The sound-money people applauded him.

Then there came to his study Professor Charles Warren, of Cornell. He was an agricultural economist. But, like all farm saviors from the time of Solon, he played with the subject of money. He had concocted a theory that the prices of commodities move up and down with the price of gold. He had written a book to prove this theory. I have read that book with care, and if it proves anything it proves that Professor Warren was wrong. Warren's theory was that by raising the price of gold we can raise the price level. Ushered to Roosevelt by Morgenthau, whose knowledge of money economics was about the same as Roosevelt's, Warren explained his theory. Along with his theory about gold control of prices went the Fisher theory of the variability of gold prices and the instability of the dollar founded on gold. Fisher had a theory of the compensated dollar based upon a commodity base instead of a gold base. These theories can be fused, but there is also much that is contradictory in them.

In any case they meant a complete revolution of our money system, utterly at sea with all Roosevelt's existing impressions—for he had only impressions. His lack of knowledge did not terrify him. It took only a few conversations to convince him—indeed, not merely to convince him, but to sell him the whole package.

Beyond doubt what sold him the theory was the thesis

that farm prices are fixed in the international market; that foreign buyers to buy our wheat must first buy our dollars; that the more dollars they can buy for their gold, the more wheat they can buy with their gold; that by raising the price of gold, gold will buy more dollars, and the whole process will end with the purchasing power of foreign buyers being increased in our market. He went on the air in a fireside chat. He delivered one of those cooing addresses. He had dictated a very rough collection of ideas on the subject. It was turned over to Raymond Moley and some others to put in final form. And there we had the spectacle of the whole admiring nation sitting at their radio sets listening to a man read a speech containing revolutionary changes in money policy—ideas which had been hastily sold to him by one group of men—handed out in phrases smoothly molded for him by another man who didn't even believe in the ideas he was reducing to phrases, while the humble masses, thinking they had found a new savior, listened in wonder, "and still the wonder grew that one small head could carry all he knew."

That was in October 1933. The price of gold was changed from $21 to $35 an ounce. The President raised his voice into the mike while the listening farmers glowed with glee: "If we cannot get prices up one way *we will do it another way.*" This, he said, is a step in the direction of a managed currency. Within three months the whole scheme was recognized as a ghastly fizzle. But from that day to this our Treasury has stood in the money markets of the world offering to buy gold at $35 an ounce. Hence we have been getting all the gold. We had $8,234,000,000 when it started. We have $19,000,000,000 now—over three fourths of all the gold in the world. We have raided other nations of their gold. We have weakened the currency of every nation in the world—our customers. And if some means is not found to stop it, we shall face a world currency crisis that will be the direct fruit of this amazing impulse.

As an example of the President's looseness of thought about such grave matters—his light-mindedness—sometime later Senator Borah and other silver senators called on him to do something about silver. They had difficulty in getting him to come down to brass tacks—he regaled them with stories. Finally they persisted in talking turkey. The President threw back his head and laughed: "Well, why not?" he exclaimed. "I experimented with gold and that was a flop. Why shouldn't I experiment a little with silver?"[1]

[1]Related to the author by the late Senator William E. Borah.

VI

Roosevelt's Big Gun

In view of these astonishing failures, what was the secret of the President's immense popularity and his devastating defeat of the Republicans in 1936?

The answer, of course, is extremely simple. Since March 4, 1933, Mr Roosevelt has had in his hands, to be spent almost at his own will, *twenty-two billions of dollars* for recovery and relief. This does not include the money spent to run the government—all the many departments with the army and the navy. This is money, over and above all the expenses of the government, that Congress put into his hands to spend where and how he chose, to bring recovery and relief.

This sum of money is almost inconceivable to the mind of man. What is equally important is that these twenty-two billion dollars was money raised without a single penny of taxes on anyone. It was borrowed at the banks. It is all still due to the banks or those to whom the banks have sold the paper. It is the bill that the people of America owe for Mr Roosevelt's seven years and must one day find some means of paying.

The spending began with Hoover. By the time he left

office he had run up a deficit of about four billion dollars. Garner, Democratic leader, denounced him. "When we come into power," he cried in the House, "we'll give the country a demonstration in real economy." The most voluble attacks on Hoover's extravagance came from Governor Roosevelt at Albany. Huge Democratic posters in big black letters on all the billboards of the country read: "Throw the Spenders Out."

After Roosevelt was elected he told Congress:

For three years the Federal government has been on the road to bankruptcy. For the fiscal year 1931 the deficit was $462,000,000; for 1932, $2,472,000,000. For the fiscal year 1933 it will exceed $1,200,000,000. For the fiscal year 1934 [Roosevelt's first year], based on appropriation bills passed by the last Congress and the estimated revenues, the deficit will probably exceed one billion dollars unless action is taken.

He blamed the collapse of the banks, unemployment, all our ills on this deficit. He then proceeded to cut salaries 25 per cent, and on April 13, 1933, five weeks after inauguration, the Democratic leaders boasted that with all the cuts planned by the President the government expenditures would show a reduction of a billion dollars.

What actually happened? At the end of this 1934 fiscal year, instead of expenditures being cut by a billion dollars they were increased by two billion dollars. Instead of a deficit of a billion dollars that the President pictured in such horrific terms, he produced a deficit of $3,600,000,000. One can make a good argument for this deficit, but what argument can be made for Roosevelt's violent attacks upon Hoover for doing the same thing on a smaller scale?

Of course the President never, until two years ago, attempted an apology for this. His apology then was that the crisis had changed things. Of course the crisis had not changed things. It was a case of fifteen million out of work in March instead of eleven million out of work in November. The crisis had come and passed by the middle of April when he was boasting that he had cut the government's expenditures. The explanation, of course, is that, confronted with the responsibility of unemployment and not knowing what else to do, he did what Hoover did, what he had denounced Hoover for doing, and without any apology for his mistake.

What was the effect of this spending? First of all, of course, it aided the unemployed. It gave money to people to buy food. In one form or another it was inescapable. The strange thing is that Roosevelt did not see that when he was running for the presidency.

Second, it also aided business. Give $15 on Saturday to a man out of work, and the money will promptly be spent for the necessities of life. By Monday or Tuesday all of it will be in the cash registers of the merchants. Pay out $300,000,000 in a month to distressed workers and farmers, and the whole $300,000,000 will flow into the cash registers of the merchants. They in turn will hire help who will spend their pay with other merchants. They will buy goods too from manufacturers who will hire help and spend other sums for raw materials. In other words, the money, as fast as the government handed it to the poor, went into the hands of business and then began to flow around in the ordinary channels of business.

This accounted for the rise in business that was called recovery. Any government can produce a rise in business and keep it going indefinitely by pumping billion after billion into business—giving it first to the poor who will spend it with the businessman. There is no trick in this. There is nothing new about it. It is one of the oldest devices of rulers in trouble in history. It was done by Pericles in Athens before Christ, by Caesar and Augustus. It was done by kings all through the modern era; on a vast scale by Louis XIV and Louis XV. It is what has been done by Mussolini, Hitler, dictators, kings, democratic premiers everywhere.

But where did the money come from? You frequently hear the statement from unfortunate people that the President took the money from the rich and gave it to the poor. This is a strange delusion that it is almost impossible to break down. The President did not get any of this money by means of taxes. It was all gotten by borrowing it at the banks.

Thus the money aided the poor. They spent it with business, which aided business, and the President borrowed it, thus avoiding war with the taxpayers.

He can go on doing this as long as he can borrow the money, but of course that will come to an end. And when it does the nation will find itself staggering under a debt that will produce one crisis after another. America and America's children will pay and pay and pay, as the President once said, "in the sweat of every man's brow," for Roosevelt's generosity with other people's money.

It did not make any difference what Roosevelt's other policies were. Spending of borrowed money is what did the job for him. The spending of taxes would not do because the taxpayers would have revolted. If he had adopted measures the reverse of the NRA, the AAA, the money policy and all his other measures, but kept the spending, the result would have been the same. If Hoover, with his policies, had spent as Roosevelt spent, he would have brought his shy prosperity from around its corner. But Hoover could not have done it. Roosevelt himself scorched him with denunciation when he did it in a small way. It took the crisis to produce the state of mind that would permit the spending, so that the crisis, instead of making things more difficult for Roosevelt, made Roosevelt's whole spending program possible.

What effect did this produce on the mind of the people? Obviously the unemployed who were put to work first in the CWA and then the WPA were grateful for it and became very naturally an immense army to fight for its continuance and for the man who wanted to continue it. Small neighborhood merchants where these workers spent their money were equally clamorous for the spending program. Billions of dollars were paid out to farmers. I recall in 1934 asking an official in the Department of Agriculture what was going to happen in the congressional elections. He took me to a vast room filled with apparently hundreds of machines throbbing away and writing out checks for farmers by the hundreds of thousands. Huge sacks of these were going out to farmers everywhere. This gentleman said: "Look at that and tell me what chance you think the Republicans have."

Many farmers were in default on their mortgages. Mortgage brokers, mortgage lenders, title companies, banks held millions of these mortgage notes. Most of these notes were worthless. They never would be worth much again. The mortgage dealers cooked up a great movement to have the government take over these notes, but they didn't appear in the picture. To the outer world it was a great movement to save the farmers from debt. The government bought all these bad notes. That made all the mortgage noteholders happy. It made the farmers happy, and then, to make them happier still, the government loaned them more money to fix up their homes and to build new barns. When it was all over, the mortgage lenders had been bailed out, and the farmers, who had been crushed by the debt, were still in debt plus the additional sums the government had loaned them; *and the government held the bag*.

The same thing happened with home owners. Hundreds of thousands of people had bought houses from speculative builders. Many of them had owned the houses for only one or two or three years. They had bought the houses at speculative, excessive prices. They were plastered with mortgages. They were in default. The course of wisdom for these home owners themselves would have been to give up these houses, but here again the mortgage noteholders and brokers, the title companies and moneylenders who held the notes got up a great movement. It was not a movement to save the mortgage noteholders and moneylenders—it was a movement "to save our little home owners!" As a result three billion dollars of these defaulted mortgages were unloaded on the government.

The administration of this was put in the hands of machine politicians all over the country. Of course it provided an army of jobs—the New York City office alone occupies a sixteen-story building. It made the moneylenders happy; it pleased the vast army of home owners who thought they were saved. It created countless jobs. It bailed out the moneylenders, *but the home owners are still in debt,* in most cases, I suspect, on mortgages that are more than the actual value of the houses, and the *government holds the bag.* The government holds five billion dollars of these mortgages. In New York City eighty thousand such mortgages were taken over by the United States government. *To date twenty-five thousand of these homes have had to be repossessed by the govern-*

ment at an average loss of $2,500 a piece. That means that these twenty-five thousand home owners are out, but the fellows who held the mortgage notes now hold 3-per-cent government-guaranteed bonds instead.

And so it went. It is not necessary to detail or examine all the innumerable streams through which these funds flowed to millions of people. Governors of states went to Washington and borrowed countless millions for pet projects of all kinds in their states. The mayors of cities went there and got millions, in many cases to meet pay rolls, to build schools, to build roads and parks. The state of Illinois alone, for instance, has gotten over half a billion dollars from the Federal government.

And the important part of all this is that all this money was dispensed by one man—the President. Congress abdicated its ancient right to make specific appropriations. It merely voted billions to the President to be spent at his discretion. In the old days Congress used to have its pork-barrel bills—a few paltry millions every session. The congressman who wanted $20,000 for a post office or $10,000 for a fish hatchery in his district asked Congress for it. If the President wanted money he had to go to Congress. But under the New Deal all the recovery and relief money was voted to the President. Then congressmen and senators and governors and mayors and politicians everywhere who wanted money had to go to Roosevelt. And they went to him, not for $20,000 or $50,000 or a million, but for millions and in many cases hundreds of millions.

It did not matter that the President started the NRA and saw it end in a comic fizzle, that he launched the AAA and saw that peter out, that he proclaimed his great money plan to the world and then never mentioned it again, that one New Deal measure after another failed and that normal business recovery refused to reappear. To millions of Americans that was unimportant. There was the steady flow of billions, all coming from the golden hand of one man who became the symbol of a generous ruler, passing out billions that he borrowed and that one day our children will be called upon to pay.

When the depression came, the government owed sixteen billion dollars, balance on the Great War. Hoover in three years added a deficit of an additional four billion to that, and Roosevelt in seven years has added twenty-two billion dollars and proposes another three billion this year, and at this moment is talking about more billions for war. If he should leave office on the first of next January, it will be with a debt of forty-five billion dollars and a great deal more if he is permitted to carry out his present war plans. And to this must be added another five billion dollars of farm and home mortgage bonds guaranteed by the government.

The President in that first New Deal—before his election—began with the premise that there must be no spending, no borrowing. Economy was the watchword. As he improvised hastily the revised edition of the New Deal, spending was tolerated as a crisis stratagem to feed the hungry. In its next phase it became a device for priming the pump of business—a means during a brief interlude for pouring funds into the bloodstream of industry to set it in motion. But industry did not get into motion, and presently the spending flowed along without apology, in default of anything else. And also it revealed its incredible political value—bringing congressmen, political machines, mayors, governors, local bodies, county courthouses, labor, educational authorities seeking money, everybody to the feet of the Chief asking for money. After six years of spending and no sign of its end, New Deal staff thinkers began to improvise new explanations and reasons for it.

First, it wasn't spending—it was investing; investing in the health, morale, security of the nation. It shouldn't be carried on the books as spending. The deficit was not a deficit; it was an asset. It was to be obliterated as a deficit by the sheer trick of not putting the figures in the books, or, better still, writing it down in black instead of red ink.

The next defense was a plea for more spending. We had not spent too much; we had not spent enough. We must not end it; we must prepare to extend and perpetuate it. The era of private long-term investment was ended. But investment was essential to the capitalist system in a democracy. Therefore the government must take over the function of investment. A variation of this was that, as private lenders would not supply money for industry any more, the government must do it; i.e., the government must issue its bonds and with the funds buy the bonds and stocks of private corporations. The trifling item that under this dispensation private investors would put their money into all the good investments and the government would put its money into all the shaky ones that private investors didn't want, seemed to escape these new apologists. But at this point the program seems stranded. There seems to be nothing in sight but more spending.

VII

The President Goes to War

As I write this the war in Europe has reached a critical stage for the two great empires, England and France. We know that the overwhelming conviction of the American people is that we should stay out of that war. There are some who would like to help the empires as much as possible without going to war. But they are adamant for not becoming involved.

It is very important, however, to realize the existence of various groups eager for American participation in the war, if it should become evident that our participation is essential to defeating Germany. These people constitute a small minority. They are to be found in certain groups, and everybody recognizes who they are. Some of them are intriguing actively to get us in.

In this situation what must we expect to happen when we pour a set of facts and events like this into the mind of the President? What kind of result may we expect to come out of that mind?

We have merely to remember the President's general state of mind on armaments. Of course the President, like everyone, frequently protests his desire for peace. Everyone does this. And I think we may assume he is quite sincere about it.

But we must keep in mind the President's long, constant attitude toward armaments and military training. He is a lover of arms. He is above all a lover of naval arms. He is one of those men whose mind and imagination are fascinated by battleships and guns. He is also one—as frequently happens in these lovers of arms—who is disposed to be somewhat truculent in his notion of the uses of these arms. Most Americans believe that we should have arms to defend ourselves; defending ourselves means defending our country from invasion. They do not believe that we should establish interests all over the world, follow our traders around with ships and undertake to police the seas of the world for those interests. We have warned Americans to get out of the fighting zones. We have warned our ships to leave the areas of war. We have passed a law to that effect. We have voted to give up the Philippine Islands, which every military man agrees we cannot possibly defend. But the President, whatever he may seem to feel, does not agree with these views. He said, while assistant secretary of the navy:

Our national defense must extend all over the Western Hemisphere, must go a thousand miles out to sea, must embrace the Philippines and over the seas wherever our commerce may be. . . . We must create a navy not only to protect our shores and our possessions but our merchant ships no matter where they may go in time of war.

This represents his ground philosophy respecting the navy. There is a touch of the Junker in him, the jingo, who, saying, "We've got the men, we've got the ships, we've got the money too," is prepared to assert a nationalist right on every sea. He is for peace as an ideal, but he is one of those lovers of peace who is too ready to choose war as a solution of the problem.

But he goes further than this. If there is one thing that the people of America hate with all their souls it is militarism. By militarism I mean that system of compulsory military training, universal military service and national armies that has made a shambles out of Europe. To escape militarism, millions of European immigrants flowed past the Statue of Liberty to America before the Great War.

Franklin D. Roosevelt is one of the few Americans who has advocated the establishment of a national army and universal military service—conscription during times of peace. During the World War he wrote:

Is it not time that the people of the United States should adopt definitively the principle of *national government service by every man and woman at some time in their lives?* . . . I hope to see the time when national government service is not only an established fact but also one of the most highly prized privileges of all Americans. I, as a father, look forward to the time when my boys will be able to render service to their country. This means service in times of peace as well as in times of war and means service in the civilian branches as well as the military branches. *The day will soon be at hand when the army and the navy of this great republic will be looked upon by its citizens as a normal part of their own government and their own activities.*

Because this was written during the war, it may be put down to an excess of patriotic zeal, though he was urging military service in times of peace. However, when the war was over, at a Victory Dinner in 1919, he said:

While a let-down was bound to follow every great national action, I hope that there will still be some kind of training or *universal military service.* That is the surest guarantee of safety. I think this ought to follow no matter what the result of the peace negotiations.

This after Germany was crushed and at a Victory Dinner after the *war to end wars.* He was busy trying to organize a naval reserve of 150,000 men all that year. On October 11, 1919, he again proposed universal military training in the army and navy at the New York State Convention of the American Legion.

The simple truth is—though Americans have not realized it—that we have a militarist in the White House who would, if he dared propose it, establish an army, with peacetime conscription, on the European model. And we must be aware of and weigh these facts about him properly before we can understand what the conflict in Europe is doing as it races through his mind.

There is another factor of the first importance—the foundation of the President's whole regime, his spending. At the end of seven years there are still eleven million people idle, and the revival of private investment is as distant as it was in 1933. Suspension, even contraction, of government spending would be followed by an immediate economic disaster while Roosevelt is president.

But national spending becomes increasingly difficult. Because of the very nature of our government, useful peacetime projects are essentially local in character—roads, parkways, playgrounds, schools, hospitals, clinics, housing, etc. The Federal government may build them, but they have to be maintained by the local governments. Today the local governments refuse these kinds of projects. It is costing so much money to maintain those already built that the local governments are at the end of their rope. Most of them are in grave financial difficulties, cannot meet their school budgets, their welfare and highway budgets; are all wrestling painfully with the baffling problem of taxes. The WPA in Philadelphia complains that it has projects that would put thirty-nine thousand men to work immediately but that the city of Philadelphia fails to authorize or sponsor these projects. It is the same in most cities and states. Governments that spend soon arrive at a point where resistance to spending becomes imperious. The resistance comes from the conservative groups who fear taxation and inflation, but it comes also from the very difficulty of finding peacetime public enterprises on which money can be spent. That is where the Roosevelt administration is today.

When this point is reached in spending programs, there is always one kind of project left that breaks down resistance—which particularly breaks down resistance among the very conservative groups who are most vocal against government spending. That is national defense. The one sure and easiest way to command national assent from all groups for more spending is to ask it for national defense. The evidence of this is that the Congress and the nation that was howling for economy only six months ago is now talking about military budgets of monstrous dimensions. And the President of the United States can say without a whimper of protest that the manner of raising money for a seven-billion-dollar airplane program is a mere "minor detail."

However, it is not possible to get the people to consent to vast outlays for national defense unless you frighten them, make them fear that enemies are about to assail them, and this is what has now happened.

Put all of these things together—the President's love of military and naval might and display, his truculence about the command of the seas, his well-known sympathies both by blood and sentiment with England, his belief in the doctrine of collective security, his dilemma in finding means to spend money and ways of holding popular approval of spending, the rising tide of political antagonism that was generally recognized before the war began—and you have the conditions that set his mind off in the direction of military adventure.

He has been playing with this subject ever since October 1937, when the severe recession got under way. He, his State Department, his military subordinates are continuously doing and saying things of a provocative character. On October 11, 1937, before Roosevelt made his quarantine speech, he called in his admirals and asked their advice for an economic blockade of Japan in co-operation with European powers. The British shied away from this. The American people knew nothing about it. Then came the quarantine speech in which he advocated international action to quarantine aggressors. If that policy had been adopted, it would have meant that England, France, the United States and possibly Russia would have used military power to strangle Japan and Germany economically. That meant the President was actually talking about war under these euphemistic phrases.

In April 1938 Ambassador Hugh Wilson in Germany warned the Germans that it was conceivable that the United States would come into any future war, and this speech, it was reported, was approved by the State Department. About the same time Roosevelt seized two islands in the Pacific near Australia and hoisted the American flag over them. In May 1938 England and Italy proposed a pact dividing up the Mediterranean and Red Sea between them, and the President issued a statement approving this pact. Later in May, Secretary of War Woodring made a speech denouncing the European dictators. When the gunboat *Panay* was struck in the interior of China on the Yangtze River protecting three Standard Oil tankers, the most frantic efforts were made to inflame the imagination of the American people against the Japanese. This was done this time, not by Mr Hearst or the yellow newspapers, but by the State Department.

Then came the spy scares. These spy stories were not given out by subordinates but by the President himself in order to give them the greatest explosive propaganda effect. The attorney general of the United States was put in the movies to call on Americans to report suspicious cases—to spy upon their neighbors.

After the present war in Europe broke out, the President began personally, directly from the White House, to give out in his own name statements about submarines cruising along our coasts. All this could be multiplied many times to show the plain purpose of the President to fill the American people with a fear that this country was going to be attacked by Germany; that as soon as England and France were done for, the United States was next on the list, that Hitler and Mussolini were meditating invasions of South America. Assistant Secretary of War Johnson has been going around the country making speeches saying that we should provide arms for a million men and build the world's greatest navy to resist a German invasion of this country, while Senator Neely of West Virginia, speaking for the administration's so-called "neutrality" policy, said that as soon as Hitler defeated England and France "he would come to Canada with the French army in the English navy, build a Siegfried line along the Canadian border, organize Sudeten areas in German cities like St Louis and Milwaukee and reduce the United States to the fate of Poland."

All this is not being done by the munitions makers, by the war-craft builders or the economic royalists. It is being done by a Democratic administration supposedly in possession of its liberal wing and by a man who was elected to office on a platform that denounced the huge appropriations for defense by the Republican administration, then less than a billion dollars.[1]

The President has now thrown off all pretense of neutrality. But he is still trying to make people believe that the Germans can invade the United States by airplane—a proposition so preposterous that he cannot get a single military man to support it. He asks Congress for 50,000 planes. And here we see about to blossom a plan for universal military training. General Arnold, chief of the army air service, says 50,000 planes would cost $7,000,000,-000. But this would require, in addition, equipment in the way of fields, hangars, repair and supply stations and quarters for a million men. This would cost another billion dollars at the very least. The naval estimate for maintaining planes is thirty men on the ground for every plane in the air. It asks 300,000 men for 10,000 planes. It would require at this rate 1,500,000 men for 50,000 planes. This does not include 100,000 pilots. Add all this to a regular army of half a million men—and they are talking about 750,000 in Washington—and you have a peacetime force of over 2,000,000 men. What this would cost, no man can say. But it is certain that this country cannot get a peacetime army of 2,000,000 men without conscription. It has the

[1] The Democratic platform of 1932 declared "For a navy and an army adequate for national defense, based on a survey of all facts affecting the existing establishments, *that the people in time of peace may not be burdened by an expenditure fast approaching $1,000,000,000 annually*."

greatest difficulty in keeping its present small army enlisted to its authorized strength. The average American will hardly be able to get the full force of all this. But the President of the United States—who believes in a national army and universal military service—has actually asked Congress for an air force that will necessarily entail this.

Our only protection, perhaps, is that it is impossible. I have inquired among experts on this subject, and it is as certain as anything in this world is certain that we cannot produce fifty thousand planes in a year and will be quite lucky if we can produce ten thousand. This being so, why does the President ask for this fantastic number? A year and a half ago Boake Carter, radio commentator, broadcast the fleet maneuvers and described how the airplanes were demonstrating their superiority over the battleships. Roosevelt summoned Carter and gave him a "dressing down." He said the admirals complained. And he made it clear that the admirals were right. He did not share these novel notions about planes. The President is an admirals' man. He is an amateur admiral himself. He is a lover of battleships—with an old, deep sentimental passion about them like those British sea lords. He has been pouring all the preparedness money he has gotten into battleships. Now he wants planes—not some reasonable number that can be produced, but some fantastic number that cannot be produced. All this was done without very much consultation with the military chieftains who were quite at sea about it all when questioned by a congressional committee. The President has been sold this new and dramatic idea of fifty thousand planes just as he had been sold the Warren gold plan in a short conversation, just as he had been sold the vending-machine plan to put an end to retail clerks.

And then an election approaches. Americans are thinking of the eleven million people still unemployed, of the farm problem unsolved; of the utter paralysis of private investment, of the mounting public debt, of the scandals in Washington and local political machines and a score of other counts in the indictment by Roosevelt's political foes. And the war, the menace to our security, the call to national defense—all this will take the minds of our people off the failure to solve our own problems and will furnish a new excuse to spend another ten or fifteen billion dollars to return his party to power.

What is more serious than all this, of course, is that the President has been "meddling in" on the European situation for two years, and is increasing his meddling. While proclaiming himself the true neutral, he has been inching the country more and more toward active support of the two great empires. He is now the recognized leader of the war party. There is not the slightest doubt that the only thing that now prevents his active entry on the side of the Allies is his knowledge that he cannot take the American people in yet. He has said privately that he does not want to send men, will, in fact, never do it. If he went in, it would be merely with naval and air forces and with munitions and supplies. This, of course, is another example of the President's method of halfway thinking. Imagine this country going to war and then refusing to supply men to do the fighting!

VIII

The White House, Inc.

It is not possible to omit a consideration of certain personal elements. The President's family has been greatly admired by many for the resourceful manner in which its members have utilized their opportunities while in the White House. The President's immediate family had never enjoyed the kind of income essential to the demands of the Hudson River society. The President himself had never earned any sum worth mentioning until he was thirty, when he was named assistant secretary of the navy. It was not until he was nearly forty that he got his first private job with the Fidelity and Casualty Company. This gave him $25,000 a year, and he doubtless drew a goodly sum from the Roosevelt and O'Connor firm. But it was not until he moved into the White House that the chances for large earnings were opened to all the members of the family. There has been some criticism of this. The tradition of the presidency has been against it, former presidents holding that they would not treat the White House as a headquarters for carrying on private business. But the President delights in breaking precedents—boasted, indeed, in his acceptance speech that the Democratic party would break many precedents.

The earnings of James, eldest son, are best known. After leaving Harvard, where he failed in his examinations, he began to study law. In that very first year as a law student an insurance company offered him a job at $15,000 a year. The work consisted, according to James, in merely sitting at a large desk. He tells us that the company didn't fool him any. "I wasn't being kidded," he said in an authorized interview in *Collier's* (August 20, 1938), "I knew perfectly well that they were paying me for the name. . . . I was newly married and needed the money." This was 1931. The next year his father was running, and the year after his father was President. Those years he made $19,000 and $21,000 respectively. Then he formed the insurance firm of Roosevelt and Sargent in Boston. His earnings from that firm, according to his statements printed in *Collier's,* were:

1934	$37,215
1935	30,785
1936	35,700
1937	52,290

In this last year the $52,290 was split between himself and his wife. He put part of it in her name for income-tax purposes. This, of course, was not his total income, for he had returns from other sources—broadcasting, commissions on other little jobs, $10,000 as his father's secretary, etc. His insurance earnings after 1937 have never been published, but they are generally supposed to have been at least as good as in the other years. But in addition to these insurance earnings he began to draw a salary of $50,000 a year from either Samuel Goldwyn or the moving-picture industry. Taking these figures, his earnings from 1933 to date since his father has been President—and part of the time he was the President's secretary—were:

1933	$21,714.31
1934	49,167.37
1935	33,593.37
1936	44,668.60
1937	61,050
1938	50,000
1939	100,000

These are average earnings of more than $50,000 a year for a young man just starting out in life. Jimmy's thrift has frequently brought censure upon his head. For instance, he got a $25,000 fee for writing the insurance on the President Lines Steamship Company. The United States government owns 90 per cent of the stock of the company, and it has also been financed by a large United States loan. The head of it, named through presidential influence, is ex-Senator William Gibbs McAdoo, who now gets $25,000 a year as its chairman. Jimmy left his job as the President's secretary to take a position as some sort of vice-president with Samuel Goldwyn—getting $50,000 a year—at a time when Goldwyn and other movie magnates were under indictment by the Federal government. Although his place of business was in Boston, he wrote insurance policies on large business concerns all over the country—National Distillers Corporation, Associated Gas and Electric (also under government pressure), Armour and Company, Stone and Webster, Columbia Broadcasting Company, insurance on Federal cotton shipped to China by the RFC, and many others. It was something new in insurance and in presidential family behavior.

What the President thought of this, of course, he has

never said. He did, however, in the midst of these activities, put a sort of O.K. upon this by making his son a White House secretary and a colonel of marines, after which the earnings of Roosevelt and Sargent increased.

Elliott Roosevelt got $25,000 a year as president and general manager of the Hearst chain of radio stations. Elliott's first foray into business was as consultant of the Aeronautical Chamber of Commerce. It was at a time when the industry was having a good deal of trouble with the Post Office Department. A bill was pending before Congress to authorize certain concessions which the Chamber was interested in, and in the course of the debate Elliott was denounced as its lobbyist. Later Brigadier General William Mitchell, former army air chief, made a similar charge. Elliott denied it. He said that he was employed by the Chamber to organize and co-ordinate various aviation companies to put them on their feet. He was quite young and inexperienced for such an imposing service. One congressman said he got $25,000 a year, another said it was only $10,000. However, later William Randolph Hearst wanted to have four radio-station franchises transferred to him in Texas at a time when he was lambasting the President. He had to get permission of the Communications Commission, appointed by the President. He employed Elliott to get those transfers. Elliott handled the job—and with great success. He was later made general manager of the whole Hearst chain at $25,000 a year.

But of course the largest earner is Mrs Eleanor Roosevelt, who puts them all in the shade, including the President. He gets $75,000 a year as President. One year he made $38,000 on the side for a serial syndicated in newspapers. It was drawn from his book that was published later and sold for fifteen dollars a set. His term will, therefore, yield him at least $638,000. But Mrs Roosevelt has earned just about twice that much, or around $1,200,000—or will have by the end of this year.

She writes a newspaper column, writes for magazines, has written books, lectures and broadcasts and has now gone into the movies.

She has written fifty-one magazine articles and three books and has contracted for three more. Her magazine articles—which sell for one dollar a word—have brought her around $75,000. Her newspaper columns fetch $21,000 a year—more this year. Her lectures are very profitable—she charges $1,500 a lecture, but speaks for less in some places. These bring in about $75,000 a year. What she has made on her books is unknown. Her broadcasts bring from $3,000 to $4,000 apiece. She has had about 150 broadcasts. She has broadcast for Beauty Rest Mattresses, a shoe manufacturer, a toilet preparation and others and is now appearing for Sweetheart Soap. The fees from these broadcasts have aggregated about $450,000. Her total earnings are something near $1,200,000. The earnings from the radio talks she gives to charity. Of course, like most people who earn large sums, she can do what she likes with it.

Her daughter, Mrs John Boettiger (formerly Mrs Dahl), has worked as a member of the staff of *Liberty* magazine for Bernarr Macfadden, has written articles and is now writing for a Hearst paper of which her husband, John Boettiger, is publisher—a job he got after he married Mrs Dahl—where she is reported to be paid $12,000 a year. She attempted to do some broadcasting. An agent representing her sent around the following notice:

Mrs Anna Roosevelt Dahl, daughter of the President-elect, has a charming voice and most engaging personality. She is willing to appear on any commercial program sponsoring a product consistent with her public position.

The total earnings of the whole family during the eight years will amount to something over $2,500,000. This is certainly an excellent showing for a period of pronounced depression.

IX

The Politician of the Lord

Not LEAST among the gifts of fortune to Roosevelt was that
he should be misunderstood by both his followers and his
enemies. His followers glorified him as a superman, a
great, wise, powerful, benevolent friend of the people.
His enemies glorified him as a would-be dictator, contriving
with demoniac cleverness the destruction of our liberties
and the socialization of their factories and countinghouses.
In both cases they glorified him.

It would be a far easier problem for his foes if he were
this potential dictator. The country would soon take his
measure and there would be a swift end of him. But
Roosevelt is no dictator. And he has not the slightest intention of upsetting the present system. He has none of
the qualities that make a dictator. He has none of the
blazing certainty about his program that marks, for instance, a mind like Hitler's or Mussolini's. No man is capable of the ruthless march over skulls and through blood
who does not feel a burning conviction upon some few
central points and who is prepared to push ahead regard-
less of cost of opinion. Roosevelt could not play the role

of dictator because too many people would hate him and he could not endure that. He went to Georgia to purge Senator George. After making a speech against the senator, filled with innuendoes rather than direct shots, George went up to him and told him he would have to fight back. Roosevelt shook George's hand warmly and said: "God bless you, Walter!" Critics have said he likes to have yesmen around him. But in fact there is no one in the White House who is a more inveterate yes-man than the President himself. It is almost impossible to go to him with a point of view without coming away feeling that he is in complete agreement with you. This is not the stuff of which dictators are made.

But the President has the stuff that paves the way for dictators. A democratic people will never yield despotic powers to a dictator. First some benevolent person whose good intentions they respect must come along and, for perfectly good reasons, ask them to weaken those safeguards that freemen have set up through the centuries to protect them from the political tyrant. Having broken them down for their benevolent friend, the breach remains for the dictator to march through when he appears. If he comes he will be a far more assertive, self-assured, ruthless man than Franklin Roosevelt. But he will find his path made easier if not wholly possible through those breaks and cracks in the democratic processes which Roosevelt made with good intentions.

He did lose his head. And that is somewhat understandable. Roosevelt is a vain man, but not truculently vain. He made some very commendable concessions about his understanding of the grave problems of the economic world when he began. But then came the episode of the crash—that utterly astonishing collapse of everything, with all the pageantry of the inauguration, the acclaim of the people, a whole nation turning to this smiling, happy new chief; the many orders and commands he gave, most of them worked out for him behind the scenes while he was busy with the details of the inaugural parade; and then the sudden recovery of the nation's morale. He stood like a hero in the center of that historic scene. Then came the billions. Senators, officials, leaders from everywhere flocked to him to ask for money and sing his praises. I dare say a man—even though a quite ordinary one—sitting alone in his room at night, may be forgiven if he thinks to himself: "By golly! Maybe I'm pretty good after all."

The greatest disservice to Franklin Roosevelt was the 1936 election, when he carried every state save two small ones. After that the man's usefulness to the country was ended. It was this that sent him off on that fatal adventure of the Court plan. There again he proceeded as he did about the airplanes. Men had been talking about naming an extra judge or two. When someone—Attorney General Cummings—gave him a plan for *six* new judges it fired him at once, just as the suggestion of fifty thousand airplanes, however impossible, fired his imagination. It was audacious. It was spectacular. He would conquer the Court utterly. He notified the Democratic leaders in Congress like a monarch issuing orders to his ministers in his cabinet. He announced it to one of his field generals thus: "Well," he said, "I have decided *to pack* the Court." He had lost his bearings. The crushing defeat he suffered split his party and embittered him. The extent to which he has lost the confidence of his own party in Congress is not even suspected by the public.

2

The mass of propaganda, direct and indirect, planned and unplanned, controlled and automatic, by which the figure of the President has been built into heroic proportions conceals pretty thoroughly the man behind the myth. The public has been only dimly aware of Roosevelt the politician.

There has been a kind of estimate of him as a sort of admirable politician—the politician of the Lord—great and just statesman who by a miracle of divine providence is also smarter and quicker on the draw than the politicians themselves. He is seen as this godlike politician battling for the poor folks. Behind this pleasing caricature is lost the true nature of the busy politician who works in the White House.

Whether or not Roosevelt is a great politician is a point yet to be ascertained. A good politician armed with twenty-two billion dollars is a more formidable adversary than a great one armed with nothing but his cunning. But certainly he is a politician. That is, he is politically minded. He thinks in terms of political maneuver. To him most questions are political questions. A problem is a subject about which two men or two groups disagree. The way to settle the problem is to get them to stop arguing and shake hands. What is more, politics is a subject which, like war, he believes he understands. He is willing to let professors and journalists write his speeches on economics and social reform. But when it comes to politics and war —that's his game. Jim Farley has been little more than a messenger boy. The President talks about the reformer's code of public service and extols the civil service. But Jim

They do not include, of course, things like the WPA, the PWA, the payment of subsidies to farmers, businessmen, home owners, etc.—all of those numerous bureaus that pay out to the people billions of funds borrowed by the government. These are looked upon as crisis or emergency devices. These are things everybody wants to get rid of. Everyone, including the President, hopes to bring about a sound recovery when these things will disappear. What, then, are the President's great measures of social reform? Perhaps we might include the SEC and the Securities Act for the regulation of security markets. More important are the Social Security Act, the Minimum Wage Act and the National Labor Relations Board. It is not possible to think of any others.

Now there is something about the most important of these that is but little remembered—the Social Security Act, the act providing old-age pensions and unemployment insurance. I now wish to make three or four statements about this. I know before I write them that no one will believe them. I put them in italics so as to induce attention and with the hope that the reader will read them twice.

It is generally supposed that President Roosevelt put through the Social Security Act. No one will believe that he actually held it up. The Social Security Act was demanded by the people, as a result of the depression. And the demand was universal. No president would have dared to postpone it. Roosevelt tried to.

The first act, introduced by Senator Wagner, he refused to support. In 1934, almost fifteen months after he took office, a committee called on him to urge action. He temporized with them. Then the Townsend movement began to roll up powerful support. The Republicans de-

*nounced the President for doing nothing about social se-
curity, and the campaign of 1934 was approaching. Then
he named a committee to study the subject. After the election he again did nothing. Then another group of men
called on him and he told them, "The time is not ripe for
old-age pensions yet." What he could have meant, it is
difficult to say. There was not only no opposition; there
was a clamorous and universal demand for this. When the
President was finally forced to act and the committee of
experts he named reported their plan, he junked the
whole plan and sent in a half-baked and immature bill
written by an inexperienced young man that was so bad
that congressmen said they didn't know what it meant.
In the end a bill was passed, but not until 1935. And then
it had in it one of the most amazing fiscal monstrosities
in the history of government finance. It made the rates
charged the working people and their employers twice as
high as they should be. Why? In order to bring in enough
to pay for the benefits to the workers and, in addition,
provide billions of dollars to pay the ordinary costs of the
government. This was done under the guise of an old-age
reserve fund which was to accumulate until it reached the
fantastic total of 47 billion dollars. This was one of those
plausible ideas which the President, in his more or less
immature conception of finance, imagined was quite an
invention. A few days before the act was approved, this
weird idea was sold to him in a few brief conversations
very much as the Warren money scheme, the undivided
profits tax and the automatic vending machine to eman-
cipate the clerks from drudgery in a clerkless world were
sold him. This amazing reserve idea was so bad, indeed,
that the President and his secretary of the treasury, when
confronted with a movement against it last year, had to*

admit it was wrong and agree to end it. Yet the President gets credit for this Social Security Act. Honest but ill-informed people say that if he were to lose power this might be imperiled. They talk as if he had put this over in the face of tremendous opposition. The President had to be driven to this great reform.[1]

The Minimum Wage Act is another case in point. In the very first days of the President's administration the Black Bill was passed in the Senate establishing a work week of thirty hours, and it was about to be amended in the House to fix a minimum wage. There were almost no votes against it. It was an extreme bill. It offers evidence, however, of how easy it would have been to get less drastic legislation passed had the President wished it early in his administration. But the President opposed this bill. And it is a well-known fact that one reason he jumped to the support of the NRA was to defeat the first minimum-wage and maximum-hour bill that Congress was ready to pass. Had it not been for the President, a bill covering this reform would have been passed three years before it was finally adopted. I repeat that I am aware of the fact that few will believe that this is true, so perfectly has the propaganda of the President as the protector of the poor taken hold of the popular imagination.

4

But in the midst of all this nothing was done about the subject of making our economic system work. It is today as completely foundered as it was in 1933. Nothing was done about the railroads—save to continue what the Presi-

[1] See "The Social Security Reserve Swindle," by the author, *Harper's*, February 1939.

dent had denounced, lending more money, increasing the debts, putting off the evil day. In the building industry that was crushed under the weight of labor racketeering, material-dealer and manufacturer combinations to keep up prices, instead of breaking these up, the President through the NRA suspended the anti-trust laws under which they could be prosecuted and actually summoned them to Washington to make bigger and tighter combinations. The building industry is as completely in collapse today as it was in 1932. He introduced uncertainty and fear into the minds of investors first by his incredible money tinkering and his inveterate borrowing policy and second by his big talk—speeches to please the liberals and progressives, threatening things he never had any intention of doing. He called Moley at the beginning of a session of Congress and told him to get up for him a "fighting speech." When Moley asked what he wanted to fight, he said: "I want to please the liberals." While no important action injurious to business followed these fiery proclamations, they did serve to send investors into the storm cellar.

If there is one thing that the practical statesman knows, it is that he cannot keep up reform forever. A system of private profit cannot function in the midst of constant alarms. The President's course should have been to select a group of essential and realizable reforms at the outset of his administration, put them through with all the power he then possessed and then seek to lead the country back to the normal processes of its economic life. But he did not seem to realize this. The Securities and Exchange Act was a step in the right direction. But, in accordance with his "weave 'em together" policy, after putting the act through—very much weakened—he named a Wall Street speculator chairman of the SEC who for two years did absolutely nothing. He seemed to feel that, having pleased the liberals with the act, he must please the conservatives with the appointments. The wise course would have been to name the half-dozen essential fundamental Wall Street reforms, put them through and call it a day, leaving business to adjust itself to that. But he didn't do that. Instead nothing was done until William O. Douglas became chairman. But the talk of doing much was kept up incessantly. And now the commission is talking about reforms when it is too late. It was the same with the Utility Holding Company Act. That was a good act to correct reasonably the bad holding-company conditions in that industry. The act was passed in 1935. It provided for reorganization by breaking down the holding companies into smaller integrated units. It should have been enforced quickly so that the industry might take its new form and go back to work. Instead nothing was attempted until recently, when it was too late to do much.

Politics, vacillation, the eternal straining after cleverness, a mind, as H. G. Wells observed of the President, "appallingly open," open indeed at both ends, through which all sorts of half-baked ideas flow, love of the spectacular, preoccupation with war problems and the affairs of Europe, and only a dim perception of the profound problems of economics and finance that dominate our scene, good intentions mixed with confused ethical concepts—these have brought the President to the tragic point where the only thing that can save his regime is to take the country off into a war hysteria.

Seven years after he took office there are eleven million unemployed, private investment is dead, the farm problem is precisely where he found it. He put through some social reforms that the country was yelling for. But these social reforms have to be almost completely overhauled. As for recovery—the President has not one plan. The cost of all this has been twenty-two billion dollars, all yet to be paid.

If it has all happened that way, it is because Franklin D. Roosevelt is that way.